Where The MEAN GIRLS Go

The Complicated and Hurtful Relationships Between Women

Laura Downey Hill

Where the MEAN GIRLS Go

The Complicated and Hurtful Relationships Between Women

©2023 Laura Downey Hill

print ISBN: 979-8-35090-464-2

CONTENTS

INTRODUCTION

To the woman who hurt me,

It has been a painful journey, some sleepless nights and heartfelt talks with friends trying to understand what I did that deserved such wrath. Yes, friendships end; we grow apart, move on, change, find new interests, and make new friends, but there is no way to understand the betrayal. I was profoundly hurt and embarrassed, but nothing could prepare me for the delight you took in wounding me.

Never worry; your secrets, insecurities, and personal disappointments will forever be safe with me. I will always cherish our friendship for what it was because I value myself. I will not say that I am stronger because of this; I am a warrior and I always will be. You have become one of my life's lessons.

People who know nothing about me took your cue. But again, do not worry; I am comfortable with the gossip of those who do not know me. You do, and in that lies the true betrayal.

Love,
Your old friend

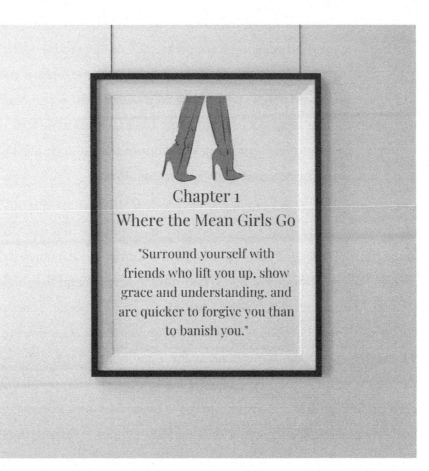

Chapter 1
Where the Mean Girls Go

"Surround yourself with
friends who lift you up, show
grace and understanding, and
are quicker to forgive you than
to banish you."

I grabbed a table right in the middle of the busy restaurant; maybe I wanted to be totally enveloped by the buzz from the tables hugging in around me; maybe I secretly wanted to be sure everyone saw me with girlfriends, chatting and laughing. The charming little pizza and wine bar was a cool spot to be seen; every town has a place like this. Eclectic sofas and mismatched chairs cozied up to round wooden tables, with a black and white hexagon tiled floor designed to look old and oversized art hanging from every inch of the cloth-covered walls. Sinatra tunes punctuated the noisy lunch crowd. A place you would love to sit and people watch, but even better to be seen – seen with friends. The table was a statement; I was not an interloper, I belonged. I was part of a growing community, a volunteer, a PTO mom, a business owner, and a city councilmember.

I grew up always being the new kid. It seemed like I would finally make friends only to have my parents announce that dad was being transferred, again. My childhood memories do not include old friends. Two elementary schools, two middle schools and two high schools. My parents even moved while I was away at college. I had to google the towns I lived in to see what the names of my schools were. The constant moving does not allow for meaningful connections, so why invest in the short term? You will always end up disappointed. I grew up being a worrier. Would we move before summer sleepovers, birthday parties, homecoming dances, football games, graduation? The only yearbooks I have are the three that mark the longest I ever went to one school. By the time I got to Cumberland Valley High School in Mechanicsburg, Pennsylvania, I was entering the 10th grade. Now as I flip through those old high school yearbook pages, the 2x2 pictures of my classmates draw a blank – until my eyes settle on one of the mean girls. We never forget the mean girls. They grow up, move on, and move away. And just like that, I realize – I know where the mean girls go.

It was Friday so the restaurant was pulsing to a sound all its own. I felt excited anticipating the great hour and a half ahead. The usual greetings echoed all around as colleagues and friends rushed in to join their lunch dates. Noticing the clinking of wine glasses, my eyes drift over to a table of three young women in cute tennis outfits toasting to a match well played. A fourth player snaked hurriedly through the packed room reaching the table, full of apologies for running late. The waiter drifts from their table to ours. Two ice teas, sweet with extra lemon, a diet coke and one large pizza with everything on it; hold the anchovies. Those first ten minutes are full of laughter as we catch up; it has been too long. Note to self, it is always too long between making time to relax with friends. Our boys were in high school together, good friends. Conversation slowly rolled from kids to sports, to grades and college trips. Our large pizza was delivered at the same time as the pizza for the cute tennis moms. At our table we immediately reached to grab a piece; our hands did a dead stop; plain cheese?! There is no way we would ever waste calories on a plain pizza. The waiter realized the mix-up and quickly scrambled to retrieve the errant pizza before anyone grabbed a slice. I looked over and noticed that the tennis gals had not made any movement toward our pizza; they were head-to-head in serious conversation. Yes, I stared; I was watching our pizza, closely. It was obvious that their conversation had shifted to more serious matters. Yes, nosey me was wondering what they were discussing. All I could gather was the leader of the group was angry at some poor 'her'. Our large pizza with everything, hold the anchovies, finally arrived. We were quick to reach for a slice. I asked for another diet coke as I heard the next table tell the waiter that they were ready for another bottle of wine. One of the gals pushed back from the table announcing loudly that she was headed to the lady's room. She turned to remind her three cohorts, "We are done with her; I never liked her anyway. You need

5

to stop calling and texting her." My girlfriends froze as we each raised our eyebrows, secret language for 'this is getting good.'

Whatever had caused the offense was not up for discussion. Obviously, this was not the first time they had been given marching orders. I felt like I should be nodding too; the final sentencing had been delivered. My friends and I drifted back to our conversation and lost track of the saber rattling at the next table. Forty-five minutes later chairs started scraping the tile floor and rushed voices at their table announced it was time to get in the carpool line. The second bottle of wine was finished; the pizza was missing a single piece. Who does that? Who wastes a whole pizza? Yes, in the back of my mind I wanted to ask for a to-go box. And yes, I was certainly judging the liquid lunch. As the ladies passed our table, two of them smiled ever so slightly at me and nodded in recognition. I knew them in passing; many might consider them cool girls. I wondered what people would think if they were privy to their treatment of 'her'? Childhood playground memories flooded back. Three of them are followers; the leader is a mean girl – all grown up.

Women can be very cruel to other women. We have all been left out, not picked, not invited. We have been the subject of giggling and pointing. Mean girls are not solely guilty of the occasional snub or slight. There is purposeful planning that seems to define mean girls; they appear to lack empathy but worse they relish causing discomfort and emotional anguish in others, and it always is aimed at other women. Yes, for a split second, I wanted to say something, admit my eavesdropping, and defend poor 'her' who would never see the ax fall. She had crossed a mean girl. But I said nothing. I simply made a mental note, this was a group of women I would try to avoid. One of my girlfriends said, "Now I know who not to mess with." We left our lunch still chatting and looking forward to our next time together. When we hugged goodbye, I sensed that we valued our friendship a little more. A poor woman named 'her' reminded us how important female friendships are. Surround yourself with friends who lift you up, show grace and understanding, and are quicker to forgive you than to banish you. I had grabbed that table in the middle of the restaurant because I wanted to show off my friendships; instead, I witnessed how mean women can be. Years later our paths would cross again, but I would be ready.

As a much older and wiser woman, I have watched the ebb and flow of friendships. Some were my own; some were others'. Once or twice, I have been stuck in the middle of a girlfriend dustup. Tread carefully if you get involved with a group of three! Through decades of business, volunteering, raising kids, and serving as an elected official, I have often felt transported back in time to the playground where awkward girls like me tiptoed around the mean girls. It is a dynamic that is real. It is as old as time. Girls love cliques but often the price of admission is following the leader's rules – always. The cohesiveness of the clique forms an invisible barrier that the uninvited girls dare not cross. Protecting the group means protecting the power structure; every member has her role and with it comes clout. I was always one of the girls on the outside who desperately wanted to be invited in. It never happened, not even once. My clique became the wannabes – ironic! If you cannot get in the group, form your own. I believe in that still today. I have many adult friends who were that same girl as me. There were many more of us on the outside than those on the inside. Now that the years have gone by, we laugh at our methods for trying to infiltrate. No one grew up without coming face to face with a mean girl.

Mean girls exist, it is a fact, and it is often a learned behavior. Whether your first encounter was at 10, 15, 20 or 50, we have all gotten in the crosshairs of a mean girl. When I was growing up, every kid in school knew who they were, and so did the parents. Decades later, when my own children were in school, parents started using terms like spirited, overactive, precocious. A new generation of parents who did not want their child's mean behavior to reflect poorly on them found it easier to make excuses than deal with the problem. Mean was just a phase, until it became their normal. I had a friend who excused every mean thing her daughter did blaming it on the fact that her daughter was an only child. When too many other parents started to push back, the child was transferred to a private school. For months the gal praised her daughter's new school; her daughter was ahead of her peers in maturity. She had been bored in public school. Well at least according to her mom. Then one day the private school called. Her daughter was a bully. Today bully is the word everyone runs from; again, parents make excuses, blame it on a phase or, whenever possible, it is someone else's fault. By excusing mean behavior, we are giving kids a pass. If as parents we cannot admit to the small things and try to fix them, how will we ever deal with the big things? Take the blinders off; stop making excuses when your children are young and more easily corrected. Yes, kids do bad things, the wrong things, sometimes they bully and sometimes they are mean. We as parents are responsible for calling our child's behavior what it is and dealing with it. No one will ever make excuses for your child like you do, especially their bosses and the people they will work with years down the road.

What kind of spouse, parent or friend will they be? Mean is hard to fix when it has become ingrained. Mean is judged more harshly in women, so do not raise mean girls.

Children can learn to be mean by using their temper to get what they want. If there are no consequences, the behavior becomes their 'go to' when they want something. We have all seen or been the parent whose child throws a temper tantrum in the store demanding a toy after the parent has said no, only to relent and buy the toy to stop the stares. Who cares what other people think of you. This is a short-term fix that can cause long-term distress. Parents teach their children by how they talk and act in front of them, such as spending time on their cell phone talking angrily about someone when kids are close by. It can be taught by constantly excusing bad behavior or pointing blame at someone else. It can be taught by allowing your child to treat another child poorly. You are constantly setting an example; yes, little is private in today's world. I am sure we have all seen a mom pushing a grocery cart with her phone to her ear in a heated debate while their child sits in the cart, absorbing the entire tone of the conversation. How many times does it happen in the car now that our phones are connected to us everywhere we go? Parents do too much and say too much in front of their children.

When I was mayor, a young girl in the 11th grade at our local high school came to a 'Meet the Mayor' event at a local business. She asked if I had a minute so she could show me something. It was obvious that she was upset. I walked her over to the edge of the event, and she showed me a screen shot on her iPhone. It was a horrible thread from a local Moms page on Facebook. I had just started to read it when she whispered, "That's my mom. She posts mean things all the time. I have lots of screen shots. Kids have started to comment at school about my mom; what can I do?" My advice was to invite her mother for a cup of coffee at her favorite coffee shop. Find a quiet spot. I suggested she be honest and let her mom know that people take screen shots, and even private groups are not private. Be kind and respectful. Let your mom know how it affects you; that is all you can do. I gave her my contact information in case she ever needed to talk. Weeks later she reached out. Her mother's initial reaction was irritation; she resented 'teens' taking screen shots of her comments and sharing them. She demanded to know who was doing it. The young girl ended up being the one who apologized. I do not know her mom personally; all I know about her is how dreadful she is on social media. Her mom, sad to say, is a mean girl. Mom is fortunate that, despite herself, she has raised a very kind hearted daughter.

Too often mean girls grow up to be mean women who do not know how to value friendship because they have learned to be self-centered. For them friendships are strictly transactional; there has to be something in it for them. It is too hard for mere mortals to live up to their expectations. As a result, they usually go through friends like water. They love bomb new friends, doing everything together, constantly talking and texting. They brag about their new 'find' to everyone in their current posse, posting picture after picture to prove the commitment. You are never respected by a mean girl; you are anointed, but you will only be worthy of the showering of attention if you follow her rules. Women like this hold friends to an unmaintainable level. It never ends well because friendship, like life, is never perfect; its value is in its imperfection, the rough edges, and torn pieces.

Mean girls cannot weather storms. As soon as it is not all about them, they are on to someone new. Popularity, allegiance and attention are the food they dine on. By virtue of always being the ringleader, they do not understand how it feels to be the one pushed away, ignored, left out. Parents, when your girls are young, do not make the mistake of getting caught up in the popularity trap. Maintaining that spot at the top can have an emotional price tag that handicaps your daughters' relationships with other women the rest of her life. The best a parent should strive to do is to prioritize kindness, humility, and empathy. Regardless of whether your child is part of the in-crowd or not (and most are not), high school and college will come to an end and life will be about who they are, not who they were back then. Understanding how to be a good friend and how to be emotionally vulnerable is a vital life lesson. Mean girls who grow up to be mean women will only attract female 'friends' who do not expect better. Unfortunately, there will always be girls who accept the rules because they learned on the playground what happens to those that do not. Mothers, it is up to us to raise compassionate women. Whether our own daughters, our daughters' friends, or relatives, we always need to seek opportunities to mentor young women. Women need healthy friendships with other women to live their best lives and to be contributors to future generations of female leaders.

Popularity is such a girl thing. Let's face it, most of us have not lived it, but we have watched from the outside. I asked the mother of a very popular girl if she too had been popular growing up. It seemed like a logical question. The mom was an expert in all things "kid social." She hosted everything, planned everything, decorated for everything and attended everything. How exhausting. Her answer to my question? "No, believe it or not, I was the nerdy girl and never had any friends. I am making sure high school is something my daughter always remembers because I don't have any good memories." Believe it or not? I absolutely believe it! If I was exhausted just watching her overcompensate, how must she feel shouldering all that self-inflicted pressure? What must her daughter think about the amount of effort needed to be popular? My friends with much younger children tell me that there are popular girls in elementary school! How do you maintain that for 12 years? It seems that we are categorizing our girls at younger and younger ages. With that comes heartbreak when your daughter is not invited, not picked, not included. Everything is out of whack when kids can no longer just be kids. Certainly, life is full of slights; they are an important part of growing up, but what happens when the line is crossed, and slights become purposeful? Mothers, the worst thing we can do is be part of the meanness; it sets a horrible example for your own children and anyone else in their friend group. What if it happened to your child?

A friend shared a heartbreaking story with me about her 5th grade daughter. A month after the school year started, one of the girls hosted a birthday party. All the girls in the class were invited. The party was held at a nearby roller-skating rink. Six girls in the class were able to attend. The mother of the birthday girl told my friend that she was happy to drop her daughter back home after the skate party. The SUV pulled into their driveway and as her daughter jumped out, she could hear all the laughter. Soon she would find out what was so funny. On Monday morning the birthday girl gathered with five of her party guests; there were hushed whispers, giggles and finger pointing. When my friend's daughter moved toward the group, everyone got painfully quiet. There was obviously a secret they were dying to share. As little girls always do, one of the girls spilled the beans on the playground. It turns out that skating was just the first half of the party; after dropping off my friend's daughter, the chosen five headed to the birthday girl's house for a sleepover. The birthday Mom told the girls to keep the sleepover a secret. That afternoon a little girl got off the school bus and fell into her mother's arms sobbing. Seriously, what adult thinks anything about that is kind? What a horrid lesson that mother taught her daughter. I wonder if the mothers of the other girls ever found out. What an ugly thing for all those 5th grade girls to witness.

Why should we care where the mean girls go? Because we end up working, volunteering, and socializing with them, our daughters befriend them and our sons marry them.

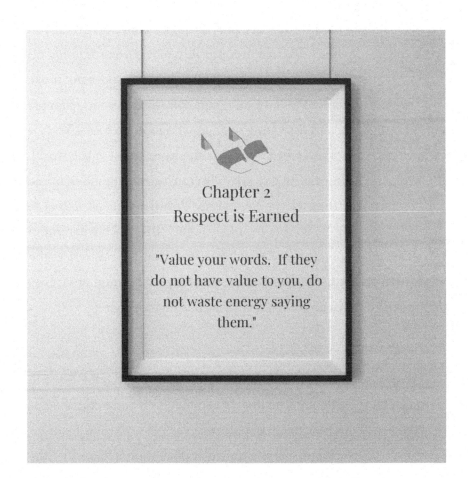

Chapter 2
Respect is Earned

"Value your words. If they do not have value to you, do not waste energy saying them."

How you act, how you speak, the courtesy you show others reflects how much you value yourself. Be thoughtful before you act, especially when you are not at your best. Do not confuse how you see yourself with what others think of you. They only see your actions and hear your words. For that split second in time, they only see what you choose to show them. I have heard too many women, young and old, say, "I don't care what other people think of me." Who do you think you are fooling? That cannot possibly reflect what is going on inside your head day in and day out. Making excuses does not make your actions invisible. We have an obligation to set a good example for our daughters and for young women who look up to us. Yes, we all have bad days, days when you leave the house mad at the world. If you cannot hide away all day, take a breath, turn on uplifting music and resolve to get through the day calmly. Promise yourself a treat at the end of the day. Soak up some crazy reality TV which will remind you that things could be worse. Be sure that your actions reflect the impression you want to make. Here are simple common courtesies that speak volumes about what you are putting out there:

1. Be on time.

   When you do not value other people's time, eventually they will move on to someone who does. Every decision you make sends a message about how much importance you place on your relationships – family, friend, acquaintance or professional. Consider the message you send when you are never on time, constantly need to reschedule, are always in a rush to leave and, when you are present, you are distracted.

   For four years I went to the same hair salon, once every six weeks on the same day of the week, same time. It fit perfectly into my schedule and kept the gray at bay. For four years I was always on time and only cancelled (if I ever did) with plenty of notice. Going to the hairdresser is a treat. No way I am going to miss an appointment, barring an emergency. The first three years were great; then things started to change. Gradually I noticed I was waiting longer and longer in the waiting area before my appointment. Ten to fifteen minutes consistently, a few times, fifteen to twenty minutes. I started paying attention to see who came out to pay right before I was called back. It was always the same lady. Was anyone else seeing the pattern? Obviously, this new gal was on the exact hair schedule as I was. I asked my stylist what was up? Was the new gal running late or was the salon? She apologized, the new client was constantly late and very demanding. The female owner did not want a confrontation, so she was trying to decide what to do. Fair enough, I trusted the owner would figure out how to handle her client. I was wrong. My stylist started rushing during my appointment to make up for the late start. I felt cheated but I am sure the client after me was happy. Hope springs eternal: I continued to arrive on time and 'late lady' continued to arrive late. The salon thanked me profusely for my patience! Who said I was patient? They gifted me shampoo and scented soap. Finally, the owner asked me if I would be willing to switch days. Their misguided efforts to pacify everyone, pacified no one. I never went back. They saw no value in my time by accepting a client who saw no value in theirs. Are women who are habitually late self-aware? Do they forget to check their calendar? Do they overschedule? How can anyone be late all the time? I believe they live life late. I think it is learned behavior that demonstrates loud and clear – zero consideration for others. Truthfully, it is a statement that you are the most important person in the room.

I was invited to sit on a panel at a corporate luncheon. The topic was women in leadership, work life balance. The event sponsor requested lunch with the panel members prior to the event to get to know everyone. One of the ladies selected for the panel has a notorious reputation for being difficult to pin down (unless she needs something from you) and after finally committing, she is always late. After a week of group texting, a date, time, and location were determined. Did I mention she had her secretary texting for her because she was too busy? On the day of the lunch at 12 noon, seven ladies were seated at a local restaurant, enjoying pleasantries, and perusing the menu. Well, everyone except her. She did make it; at 12:23pm, something came up. Everyone glanced uncomfortably at our host when she blew in, well everyone except me. It was not my first rodeo with her. She arrived out-of-breath, her over the top apologies changed the whole conversation to, you guessed it, her. It is her reality, the way she operates day in and day out. She gets away with it because people are too polite to push back. She is in a position of leadership and has the opportunity do amazing things, but people talk, and they talk first and foremost about her disregard for other people's time. Being habitually late becomes a message heard loud and clear. You value your own time more than you value other people's time. Yes, she was late for the event but because of her position excuses were made and the program schedule was slightly rearranged. The other women on the panel, who were all on time or early, made a mental note. When she is involved either take a pass or know what you are signing up for.

2. Do not make promises you never plan on keeping.

    You know who these women are; we all do. You volunteer with them, do business with them, attend church, and go to lunch with them (if they do not cancel). They are always full of joy and praise when they see you and are the first to offer their help and support. "Please call me and let me know what you need!" Yes, always said with an exclamation. You remember their offer because they go out of their way to make sure you do. So, what happens when you call to let them know what you need? Crickets. They are all about the good feelings in the moment, never thinking past the promise. Their promise has no more weight than commenting on the weather. They are so wrapped up in their own world that they never consider that the people they make commitments to are counting on them to keep their word. If you are a woman who never comes through, stop saying you will. It will save you so many awkward moments (assuming that you care). Stick to talking about kids or the weather. A broken promise, large or small, is still a poor reflection on you. Value your words. If they do not have importance to you, do not waste energy saying them.

3. Do not be a constant asker and never a giver.

    In my community, like most, volunteers are always pleading for donations. Whether it is fundraising for the PTO (Parent Teacher Organization), kids' sports teams and clubs, charity galas or numerous worthy causes, we all hate asking and being asked. I still remember, years ago, when my mom and I filled my little brother's red wagon and went door to door in New Carrollton, Maryland, selling Camp Fire Girls peanuts. I hated ringing the doorbell; I hated asking. My salesman dad would walk with me on Saturdays which added the pressure of what he called 'closing the sale.' As a result, my entire adult life I have had a soft spot for Girl Scout cookie season. For years I bought dozens of boxes and brought them to my office to spread the love and the calories. These days

I know better; I will eat half of them (especially the shortbread) before they get to the office. But I will always support their effort. Now I am quick to donate cash or scan the QR code as I pass their cookie table at my Tom Thumb grocery store. I smile considering all the calories saved. Not every donation is as easy to justify as a box of cookies, or as affordable. Few of us can give to everything all the time, so yes, we must choose, but I have found that there is 'giving etiquette.' Some understand it and others do not. Do not say you will donate if you will not. Do not be a constant asker if you are never a giver.

I feel badly for businesses, especially small local businesses caught in the trap of always having to say yes. It is a conundrum. They need their name out there supporting events, but the constant 'asks' to give can be a stressor, especially when their livelihood depends on the support of the community. Unfortunately, they get stretched thin especially during difficult economic periods. If you are taking donated goods or services from a local business, support that business and ask your friends to support the business. Be loud about it. Take it upon yourself to spread the word and make sure the business knows it. Giving and taking must be a two-way street. Raffle items, silent auction items, live auction items – donations, donations, donations. Do not be the woman who pleads with friends for your causes but hides when others are pleading for theirs. I know a woman who is so impassioned by her own charitable work but goes underground if she thinks you want a donation from her. She does not return calls, emails, texts, hibernating until the coast is clear (or your event is over). She will be around next year right on time asking for a donation.

I will see her coming a mile away and I already know what she will say, "Oh my gosh it's so great to finally run into you!! We keep missing each other. Where has the time gone? We must do lunch!" We never do.

Volunteering, fundraising, and 'asking' are vital to engaged communities and to connected citizens. Prioritize giving back in whatever way you can; it sets a powerful example. Not all giving needs to be about money; donating your time is just as valuable as your treasure. We all go through different stages in life when one is easier to give than the other. Do not promise what you cannot afford to give. When I speak to groups of young women, I urge them to get involved in community service. If girls are exposed to the value of giving back at a young age and discover how fulfilling it is, they will prioritize it as an adult. What a positive impact we can have on our communities.

4. People's time is a gift; do not take it for granted.

Like people who constantly ask but never give, do not be a woman who always leans on friends and colleagues for help and advice but is never available when that friend needs your shoulder. Do not misuse anyone's time; it is as simple as that. When you ask a colleague or friend for their time, come prepared and ready to listen. Time is a gift, so be engaged in the conversation not with your phone or looking over their shoulder. Do not schedule time if you do not have it to give. Simple courtesies that so many seem to take for granted these days. We have all wasted time with clubs and organizations that are not welcoming. I do not care if it is professional, social, or philanthropic. If it is not a comfortable fit, I move on. It is a simplistic statement, but I wish I had understood it decades ago. You deserve to be very selective with how you spend your free time. Do not give time and emotional energy to anything or anyone who never reciprocates.

For 14 years I served as an elected official in my city, Southlake, Texas. Six of those years were two terms I served as the mayor. It was not unusual for citizens to request to meet with me to discuss city issues, usually (nine out of ten times) a dispute with a neighbor or HOA, Homeowners Association. It is incredibly rewarding but there are times that leave you scratching your head. Where has common courtesy gone? I could tell a dozen stories, but one experience is unforgettable.

A citizen called town hall to request a meeting with me. I looked her up on Facebook, LinkedIn and Instagram, trust but verify. Yes, I have been ambushed by someone who showed up with a posse and a politically motivated agenda. This woman seemed legit; she had an impressive job and was active in the community – no red flags. When staff called her to set the appointment, they clarified again that it was a 'serious neighborhood issue,' her words. I knew it had to be a clash with a neighbor, probably an errant tree limb that had the nerve to drop leaves in her yard. True story. I walked into town hall about 20 minutes before our appointment. I took the elevator up to the 4th floor and there she was, early, nice. Wow, she was dressed to the nines, hair, nails, expensive leather briefcase on her lap. Maybe we were getting sued? I did a double take, then grimaced at my own outfit. It was 3pm on 'casual' Friday, and only one of us had gotten the memo. Of course, I fell all over myself explaining why I was dressed so casually. At my 'paying' job it was casual Friday and I had just run over from my office. I do not know why women always feel that they must make apologies. Note to self, get over it.

I offered her a seat and took my spot behind the oversized desk; I felt in control again. Niceties completed. She started love bombing me with compliments, what a great mayor I was, a fine example to young girls. How did I find the time to juggle every-thing so effortlessly – work, family, community? It was starting to feel like . . . a sales pitch! That moment of realization when you see the hand go for the high gloss trifold and all you can think is how do I get out of here. Yes, her whole set up was a fib. I will not say what she was trying to sell but I will tell you it was an amenity, a fun to have but not a need to have. It certainly would have cost the taxpayers a lot of money. I can only imagine the commission. Her company had purposely sent a woman sales assassin to target the woman mayor. My switch flipped; she would get 20 more minutes from me period, just long enough for me to mentally do my grocery shopping list and figure out what was for dinner. She lost my attention and my respect the moment I realized she had no value for my time. And no, she did not make the sale and all her follow-up calls to staff claiming I was 'very' interested failed. We were not friends before that meeting, and we were not friends after it but we lived and volunteered in the same community so our paths would continue to cross. I formed a lasting opinion of her based on what she might consider harmless dishonesty; I doubt to this day that she realizes.

I clicked on a phone message from a number I did not recognize. It was a woman I only knew in passing. Her tone was pressing; she wanted some advice on a child/school matter. She left a list of questions and begged for a quick call back. I called back, maybe an hour had passed. No answer, straight to voicemail. No worries. I left her a detailed message, answering all her questions since she sounded rushed to get information. She did not call back or send me a text, so I assumed she got everything she had hoped to garner from me. Two months later, yes, eight weeks, I get a text. "Sorry for the phone tag." Hmmm, I think there is an expiration date on playing phone tag!? "Can you call me as soon as possible? I have a few more questions." Yup, I called right back. Nope, she did not answer. Yup, I got a text five days later, same message about playing phone tag. I returned her text and asked her to call me in the next few days at her convenience. Nope, she did not return the call that week, or the next. Instead, three weeks later she sent another text. Are you free to talk? Nope, I gave myself permission to hit delete. My time was not valuable to her. If it could wait for two months, three weeks and five days (but who is counting), how important could it be? It was a little annoyance in the scheme of things, but she made an impression none the less, one that lasted.

Never underestimate the long-term value of honest dealings along your journey and the cost of dishonest ones. More often people form fleeting opinions from simple acts or ordinary situations. There is nothing big that you can put your finger on, but they made an impression none the less. Life is a series of normal interactions, and it is our choice how we handle them – encounter with a neighbor, a restaurant server, the bank teller, checkout clerk at the grocery store. We are constantly being judged by the little things and how we handle them.

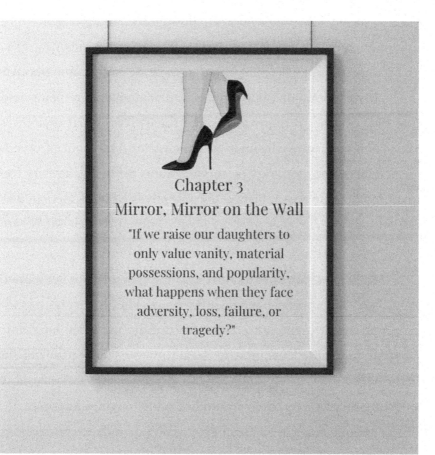

Chapter 3

Mirror, Mirror on the Wall

"If we raise our daughters to only value vanity, material possessions, and popularity, what happens when they face adversity, loss, failure, or tragedy?"

We are in a battle against a societal shift that wants to upend the role of mothers. There is a deliberate effort to strip us of our place as our daughter's principal role model. These culture corrupters lie in wait in every corner of mainstream media – advertisers who target girls, telling them what lifestyle they 'deserve,' influencers, redefining what their body should look like and how they should dress. Parts of society have made efforts to downgrade the significance of a mother's impact on the type of woman her daughter will grow up to be because it is not who they want her to be. It has become popular to challenge traditional female roles. Our daughters are being told that they do not need anyone except themselves. What matters is their happiness, wants, feelings and 'their truth.' But conceit breeds an unfulfilled life, nothing any mother wants for her daughter. Too many mothers are accepting this false narrative and surrendering their responsibility to the peer pressure of a 'community' that could care less about the type of adults their daughters grow up to be.

Mothers, we are our daughter's primary teacher, not her school, Hollywood elites or social media influencers. They learn about kindness, vulnerability, empathy, and honesty from us. They hear how we speak to their teacher, how we treat the store clerk or the barista in the coffee shop. They watch how we dress, how we socialize, how we treat other women. Being a mother is the toughest job on earth. It is not about activism or ideology; it is about guidance and lessons taught, day in and day out, by example. Children are sponges; if they are not soaking up you, believe me they are soaking up someone else. Influences, good and bad will determine the woman they become, the relationships they form and the kind of parent they will be. We owe it to our daughters to demonstrate the best and teach them to learn from the worst.

There has been an explosion of mean girls – young women growing up who do not value true friendship or meaningful relationships. We are raising too many young women who are self-absorbed and lack the ability to regulate themselves when it comes to their 'feelings.' There is nowhere else to look but in the mirror. We are teaching our daughters material pride and physical obsession. Yes, they are inundated with it every time they pick up their pricey iPhone, but parents are knowingly handing over their children's moral compass to a 6" x 3" screen and the influencers that want your child's adoration and attention. The line between want and need has blurred, because parents do not want to say no and face their child's disappointment. Too many parents want to be the friend with the credit card because it is a lot more fun to be the cool parent. Parenting is a tough job. Mothers want so badly for their daughter to be popular, smart, athletic, exceptional at SOMETHING.

It is not fair but mothers are constantly being scored by their daughters' accomplishments. We all want our daughters to fit in, to be liked, to have nice friends and achieve their goals. What if you are a mother whose daughter struggles? Without supportive friends a mother can feel isolated and overwhelmed. It is compounded by the pressure society puts on girls to look a certain way. Moms find themselves being pushed by their daughters. As a result, they bend their own rules and fall in to the trap of helping their daughter keep up with the cool girls. The shortest skirt, tightest crop top, the prom dress that shows the most cleavage. We are allowing our daughters to dress way beyond their years because we fear saying no; we want to be their friend. We want them to have friends. It is searching for the magic potion that will make our daughters all 'we' want them to be. Regardless of what part of the country you live in, just look at social media around homecoming and prom. There are so many moms that want to be the 'cool mom' that they have convinced themselves that promoting their daughter's sexuality is somehow modern.

I have met families in my own town that have strapped them-selves financially just to make sure 'Susie' has hair extensions, weekly visits to the nail salon, designer clothes, an expensive car and yes, even plastic surgery. The obsession to be popular, to stand out, to have it all (fake or not) is not the fault of daughters; it is the fault of mothers who are often afraid to say no. Wives would rather argue with their husband over an outrageous Visa bill than disappoint their daughter, who is going to die if she does not have a Gucci belt. Yes, I have had an awkward Gucci moment. The city was hosting an event honoring a group of high school juniors. Their parents were in attendance and I was making my way through the event meeting as many family members as I could and offering my congratulations. One of the young girls ran over to me with a friend. We hugged and took a selfie as they both exclaimed, "I love your belt, I want one just like it." With that, one girl turned around and begged her mom to come over "quick" to see my Gucci belt. As her mom joined us I was making the comment, "Well, I am 60 years old and this belt was a treat that I bought myself. I am sure when you graduate, get a good job, and save your money you can buy a Gucci belt too." I thought that her mother would appreciate me taking one for the team. Instead, she gave me the strangest look, I swear she started to roll her eyes but stopped herself. She turned to her daughter and exclaimed (a bit too loud), "Absolutely." I just stood there; it was an awkward moment. I have no doubt that the young girl got her $600 Gucci belt.

I purposely asked a gal I know about a picture she had posted on social media of her 9th grade daughter. I will be honest I was being nosey; I spotted the $560 Golden Goose sneakers, and I was dying to know if those belonged to her daughter or had she leant them to her (yes I still borrow clothes from my mom). The mom was humored that I would think she had leant them to her daughter. But moreover, she said, "All her friends wear them. I had to lie to my husband when he asked her about them. I told him we bought them used, 60% off. He will never know the truth." Wow, I do not know what example was worse. Buying the shoes (or else she would die) or lying to your husband, in front of his daughter. Of course, the daughter was happy to see her mom's willingness to lie on her behalf – over a pair of pricey sneakers. Lesson learned.

What kind of future leaders, spouses, mothers, girlfriends are we raising? Your daughter does not 'need' to be popular, but she does 'need' strong morals, ethics, and empathy. I was not popular growing up and I doubt many of us were. It would not be an exclusive group if everyone was invited. Society has shuffled the deck and many mothers have misplaced their moral compass, their innate sense of what is right and appropriate for their young daughters. I believe the same about mothers who see their role as pushing their daughters to the limit to achieve – with specialized lessons, professional training, the finest equipment and then dumping tons of expectations on them to not only perform but outperform.

We are teaching our children to throw money at things until you get the results you want. This is the lesson they will take into adulthood; this is how they will treat valued relationships; this is how they will raise their own children. It can lead to poor financial decisions that will follow them forever. These misguided lessons will be their map for guiding their own life choices. Our responsibility is to raise our daughters to be the best versions of themselves, confident in their decision-making and with a willingness to work hard for what they want. If we raise our daughters to only value vanity, material possessions, and popularity, what happens when they face adversity, loss, failure, or tragedy? What happens when they cannot afford the swanky things we bought them their entire childhood?

Over the last 15 years many mothers have succumbed to the constant societal beatdown. As they have surrendered, they have gradually handed over much of their parenting responsibility to schools and social media influencers – people who often do not share their values. The internet has given complete strangers access to your child. If you are not watching, they always are, and they do not believe that you are the most important role model in your daughter's life. We do not need more activists trying to redefine motherhood, telling us what a good mother looks like and acts like. Mothers need to charge back into the arena and fight for our daughters. Ultimately, we cannot talk about the world needing (deserving) more women in leadership if we are not committed to raising those women, mentoring them, showing them how to move from the sidelines and take a seat at the table. If our daughters are taught to put material wants first, vanity and popularity foremost, they will struggle as adults. Empowered women do not need or want playground cliques. They are confident in who they are, the decisions they make and the people that they surround themselves with. In order to teach our daughters to be future leaders we need to teach them these valued basics:

1. It is what is on the inside that will get you where you want to be.

2. Value who you are, not what you have.

3. Own your uniqueness.

4. Speak and act with honesty and integrity.

Teaching our daughters that their self-worth has anything to do with how many times they score a goal, what grade they get on a test, how popular their friend group is or how many invitations they receive is in effect teaching them to never rock the boat – that it is safer to be a follower. They will measure their success by how long they can hold on to the boat rather than risk reaching for the opportunity to be the captain.

We risk raising mean girls if, as grown women, we do not learn how to be less hypercritical and show more grace to each other. Mom shaming results in many moms trying desperately to keep up, overspending, over giving and relaxing their own principles in hopes that their daughter will be one of the cool girls. We have done our daughters a huge disservice by oversexualizing them. Women fought for generations to be judged on the content of our minds not our bras but here we are again and this time it is of our own doing. Even in my own social media circles mothers get love bombed with the outpouring of compliments every time they post a provocative, dolled-up picture of their teenage daughter. Friends feed the beast with comments like, "She looks like a model." "She looks all a grown up." "Wow you must be so proud." (Seriously that should be a question not a statement.) Your 16-year-old daughter in a painfully short skimpy dress and made up to look 28 is something to be proud of? When your daughter spends her entire evening pulling her hemline down and her neckline up, there is a problem. Then we turn around and put them in a room with a bunch of pubescent knucklehead teenage boys and demand that no one sexualizes our daughter. What could go wrong? Mothers need to wake up.

Society has become so self-absorbed, prioritizing our own feelings, following our own truth, demanding that everyone operate in a way that does not offend or trigger us. If we, as women, do not take back ownership of motherhood, what chance do our daughters have? What will future generations of women look and act like? Do we honestly think they are going to have the interpersonal skills and self-awareness to form and maintain meaningful adult relationships, raise happy children, and become successful members of their communities? Our responsibility as the mothers of daughters is to raise strong young women who are resilient. These young girls will be tomorrow's wives, mothers, business owners, bosses, and community leaders.

Being a mother is an awesome responsibility. The mother daughter relationship is like no other. We teach our daughters tenderness and affection by being the person they come to for hugs, the person who is there when they are sick, lifts them up when they are down and holds them closer when they reach their goals. We hurt for them, and they feel it; they sense how much we care and learn to model it. We are their first feminine role model. Let them see you cry. Share your dreams, mistakes, and disappointments whenever appropriate. You are teaching them that life is not perfect, and we do not always win, more importantly the world does not revolve around our wants and desires. We teach our girls to be nice girls, not mean girls, by how we handle situations when things do not go our way. None of us will ever have 100% good days. We must always be cognizant that what we are putting out there is what they will absorb. Mothers will have bad days and we will make missteps. Never be afraid to apologize or explain your poor behavior to your children, especially when you have made the mistake in front of them. Do not make excuses, take responsibility. It is a valuable life lesson.

I have had several opportunities over the years to apologize to my children for being unnecessarily impolite. In 2015, I was in a political race for mayor of my city. Campaigning day in and day out for months will wear you down. As someone who is normally grouchy with less than eight solid hours of sleep, plus constant meetings, greetings and smiling, I was totally stressed out. I left the house some mornings looking for someone with whom I could be aggravated. It could have been the bank teller, a slow driver in the fast lane, one of my employees. Yes, I was just daring someone to unknowingly cross my path.

My dry cleaner was in the wrong place at the wrong time. I have used the same dry cleaner for over a decade. I have never had a single complaint, until I went looking for one. After picking up a clean and ready to go campaign wardrobe for the next week's events, when I got home I realized that my red dress, was 'missing.' Not a big deal, of course I say that today after eight hours of sleep and the campaign years over. But on that day, I was furious. I stomped around the house yapping at my kids and husband about the earth-shattering blunder. I acted like it had been done to me on purpose. Yes, this certainly makes me look ridiculous, and I am surprised I am sharing it. I complained all weekend and vowed to go in Monday morning to demand they find what had now been elevated to 'my favorite dress.' Monday morning, I drove to the dry cleaners. I was impolite and patronizing. As I write this, I hope my memory is foggy; maybe the years have made it seem worse than it really was, praying so. But it was bad enough that I still remember eight years later. They were very polite and promised to look again but checking their computer, they assured me that I had not dropped off a red dress (my favorite). I begrudgingly agreed to check back in a few days. Then I threw down the decisive 'Karen' threat, "I will be finding another dry cleaner." I was like a dog with a bone. I could not let it go and I am sure my family was fed up with my silly obsession.

The dress was gone, until it was not. I found the dress days later; it had slipped off a hanger and lay where it had fallen a week before, on my closet floor under a row of pants and dresses. Obviously it never made it to the dry cleaners. I stood there frozen; I had said so many weird things, all over a dress, all because of my own mistake. I had lost control over a dress??? I was so embarrassed. My first thought was to never mention the dress again. I could certainly not go back to the dry cleaners (too humiliating). I could never wear the dress again; it will have to go upstairs, hidden in my 'fat clothes' closet. Maybe I could sneak it out of the house and donate it. Seriously? I was acting like I had committed a crime.

I walked out of my bedroom and put the crumpled-up culprit on the kitchen table. I waited until, sure enough, one of my children wandered in and did a double take. Yes, I confessed, but went further to admit what a jerk I had been to the dry cleaner. I asked if anyone wanted to come to the dry cleaners with me to hear my apology; no one did. I was on my own as it should be. It was a valuable lesson. I told my kids that I promised to get my emotions under control. Now that was something with which the entire family agreed. Do not be afraid to share your shortcomings with your family. Share the good, the bad and the ugly whenever it is appropriate. Eight years later, I still use the same cleaners. Yes, it took months for me to stop apologizing every time I dropped off clothes.

We are in a cultural crisis that threatens the traditional role of mothers and daughters. If your daughter does not have a strong support system with you as a vital part, she is a target. Outside influences seek to convince young women that they do not need family role models, mentors, or close relationships. That is why our responsibility as mothers has never been more important than it is right now. You establish trust at a young age by setting boundaries that reflect your families' beliefs. Accept that there will be disappointments because setting boundaries means that sometimes you have to say no. Many generations of women fought for the empowerment we enjoy today. As mothers we must do better for our daughters because they are the future.

Chapter 4
The Lonely Hours

"A nonstop schedule can actually be very isolating. You must have downtime, time that allows you to breathe and spend time with people who fill you up."

B USY. When did everyone get 'too busy.' Busy has become the excuse for dropping the ball and every other 'oops I forgot' that comes along. Growing up, I do not remember BUSY being the mantra it is today. These days everyone is always too busy; just accept it. It just flies out of people's mouths without any thought. And seriously?

What are you supposed to say to that? There is not a comeback; it ends the conversation. Accept it and move on. I have a friend who never misses the latest binge-worthy show on Netflix, but every time I talk to her the first thing she says, without exception, is, "I am so busy I do not have time for anything anymore." I have always wondered how she wanted me to respond; I say nothing. I certainly do not begrudge anyone free time in front of a good Netflix binge but let us be honest, we make time for what is important to us. Stop promising to do things if:

1. You do not want to do them.

2. You do not have the time to do them.

3. Both.

It is okay to say no and honestly, if 1,2 or 3 apply, you should. Habitually dropping the ball reflects negatively on you and what people think of you. If you are invited to an event, RSVP honestly. Do not sugar coat your availability because you have good intentions. Do not beg for an invite and then no show! This is actually a thing. People are planning, spending money and time based on your response. Thank you to those that take the time to RSVP, even if it is a No. When did this become optional rather than good etiquette? I guess it has gone the way of thank you notes. I know a woman (we all do) who RSVPs yes to everything and never makes it to anything. Something always comes up because, yes, she is just too busy! I never count on her and would not give it a second thought except she sends a half dozen text messages profusely apologizing 20 minutes before the event starts. If you find yourself constantly apologizing, you are constantly overpromising.

Women tend to judge, and they are judging you by what you chose to put out there. You will get overlooked, not invited, and always be on the outside looking in if you are casual about your promises. Always being too busy comes across as if your life is just so much fuller than everyone else's. If you are someone who cannot be counted on, people will move on to someone who can. We invest in those who invest in us. You can develop a reputation that you do not want without even realizing it. Of course, you may be too busy to notice.

I have met countless 'very busy' lonely women. These women come in all ages. They have families, jobs, pets, volunteer work, and full schedules, but they are isolated on numerous levels. We all know women who always seem to be on the go, rushing from one meeting to the next, lunches, committees, carpooling, hours spent running in a dozen different directions. I have been that woman. A nonstop schedule can actually be very isolating. You must have downtime, time that allows you to breathe and spend time with people you enjoy. A healthy human being needs genuine friends, colleagues, and mentors. If you do not take care of yourself and prioritize the relationships that fill you up, you risk becoming okay with being lonely. Do not ever be too busy for yourself.

Maybe because I was a woman mayor and had been divorced years earlier, I often got calls from women in the community with marital problems. Some of these women I knew, some I knew of. One, who I somewhat knew, called and asked to meet privately. I invited her to come by my house. Opening the front door, I could see the tear stains on her face. I invited her in and nervously rushed to get her a glass of water; sticking a few tissues in my pocket. Painfully, she shared that she was in a lonely and loveless marriage but had no choice but to stay. Her name was not on the house, on the cars, or on anything else. They had three young children. Her husband traveled every week for business, so she had not worked outside of the home during their 12 years of marriage. They had married after her husband's senior year in college; she was a sophomore. They followed his dream and moved to the West Coast, she dropped out of college and never graduated. It is all too common, a gorgeous house, fancy cars, designer clothes and expensive jewelry; nothing that truly matters. Sadly, she was not the only woman I would sit with and just listen. So many women are unhappy, isolated, and stuck. Money may fill the piggy bank but it does not fill the heart.

Unfortunately, many women fill the void in their hearts with material possessions rather than memorable moments. Is it really a surprise that as we have amassed more material possessions, we have become a more disconnected society? I live in a city eight miles from one of the busiest international airports in the country. Because you can get anywhere in the world easily, the city attracts families from all over the USA and the world, especially people that travel regularly for work. As a result, a huge number of women are the sole parents, Monday through Friday. They are under tremendous pressure to be mom, dad, teacher, disciplinarian, and taxi driver five days out of seven, week after week, month after month, and year after year. On top of that, many of them work outside the home! I was a divorced mom raising three children on my own for several years. I was mentally and physically exhausted, and my personality was hanging by a thread some days. I give these women a lot of credit, but without real friendships, it becomes easier to pick up the laptop rather than the telephone.

Women are emotional beings and need confidants. Too many women confuse friendship with the superficial relationships easily formed online. For many it is all they have time for, for others it is all they have left. Meeting that woman in my home created a connection that would have been impossible through social media, telephone, text, email, or even zoom. Women need the physical connection, eye contact, holding a friend's hand, offering a Kleenex, giving a hug. Loneliness breeds odd behavior, especially in a hyper social media world where it always looks like everyone is living their best life. For some, the appeal of connecting on social media is a huge temptation, especially after 9pm and a few glasses of chardonnay. After dinner, homework and bedtime stories, many women take their loneliness online.

How many times have you witnessed a blowup on Facebook, Twitter, or Nextdoor. People run to the drama like moths to the flame, posting popcorn-eating memes, signaling this is going to get good. I am not on any of those pages in my own town but the minute something happens, my phone blows up with screen shots. The same 12 people are commenting; the same 150 are watching in amusement. Do not be silly enough to think that your 'private' group is private. Arguing that no one has the right to share screenshots is naïve. The habitual need to look for an online fight takes so much effort and reflects pathetically on those that constantly search for it.

Women crave emotional connections. We love having a sounding board, talking things through. You cannot work through things on social media like you can over a cup of coffee. It is a place to vent rather than resolve. Do not be tricked into thinking you have found freedom with like-minded posters. I have seen too many women ruin their reputations and truly embarrass themselves by the things they post. Yes, society is still harder on women who lose control than on men who do the same. I often mentioned in speeches that I gave while being mayor that there were a half dozen women in my community who all I knew about them were the dreadful things they said on social media. If they were standing in front of me, I would not be able to see past their disregard for their neighbors, trashing of local businesses, lies, exaggerations, conspiracies and, in some cases, abhorrent language. I doubt they even know how people look at them or what people think of them (or maybe they do not care).

Maintaining authentic friendships, especially with women, can be difficult. Women are so hard on other women and rarely extend the same level of grace as they do in their friendships with men. I have watched a woman in my town go through 'friends' like paper towels (for years), and how do I know she is on to a new best friend? Everyone knows. She reminds me of one of those large sky-piercing search lights that announce the Grand Opening of a new club or the start of the Academy Awards. But the spotlight never shines long; what mere mortal can live up to the expectations? And to quote Project Runway, "One day you are in, the next day you are out." Soon enough there is a new bestie in the spotlight. Women like this do not need genuine connections or a supportive group of friends; they need something (or someone) new to show off. I have certainly had my moment in the spotlight; many of you have too.

For my entire life, I have loved our political process and enjoyed political dialogue. I no longer do. Since my freshman year in college, I have worked the polls, knocked on doors, volunteered on campaigns, and never taken my right to vote for granted. Sadly, politics has become so toxic for many that it has ruined longtime friendships. No group, no candidate, no committee, and no elected official at any level should be placed on a pedestal. Where else in our country does the person who promises the most but produces the least win? The rabid supporters are left to run around making excuses or passing it off as 'no big deal' when they find out they really knew nothing about the person for whom they burned the house down. No surprise: we have all seen a hyena feeding frenzy on the Nat Geo Wild channel.

Social media has become the new playground for mean girls. It makes sense, what an effortless place to find followers by saying and doing outrageous things. All in the name of fighting to secure their imaginary fortress. There is a world of online groups that prey on lonely women. The pages rejoice in group think, turning on people easily and using pack mentality to justify their attacks. No one in the group will dare push back because they fear being banished, or worse, becoming the prey. They just quietly gossip offline in group texts and share private screen shots. I have never been one to live in fear of the mean girls. What makes them better than me or you? Nothing other than the power we choose to give them. People are becoming fanatically loyal to people they really know nothing about, some of whom are probably sitting in their basement wearing underwear just trying to wreak havoc.

I recently blocked a woman from my social media (well, actually several, but that's a story for later in the book; totally liberating). I knew of her before she got absorbed by the political dust devil. She was not a friend, but what I would say is I knew her through people I consider good friends. Watching her change was sad but predictable: a young mother, overwhelmed, with a desperate desire to belong. A woman who had never been part of any solutions in the past, she rarely voted, but overnight she became a keyboard warrior. She surrendered her good heart and became a sycophant. Her new 'girlfriends' often say and do awful, hurtful things, but she believes in the cause, so she makes excuses for their methods. How sad. She understands the price of admission and fears what will happen if she does not toe the line. Imagine joining a cause but being bullied to stay. Follow the rules and obey authority; sounds just like the mean girl's playbook. Sometimes we try so hard to fill a void in our personal lives that we form associations our heart knows we should avoid.

I wonder if mean girls need to be surrounded by followers to mask their own loneliness and lack of confidence. It begins on the playground, finding the little girls who desperately want to belong, knowing they will do anything to be part of the clique. We have all made the mistake of befriending a mean girl, maybe even more than one over the years. Women look for commonality in friends; we are excited when we meet another woman in our same industry or one who shares the same hobbies or has children in the same activities. We gravitate toward common interests and invest in what we hope will be a long-lasting friendship. It does not always work out the way we hoped.

A successful businesswoman who has become a good friend over the years, shared a story with me about a friendship she had with a mean girl. The friendship lasted seven years and ended almost a decade ago, but the betrayal is still raw. With mean girls there is always a non-negotiable breaking point; the problem is you never know what it is. Too often, like in this case, there was a change in the balance of their friendship. The mean girl could not tolerate the shift. They met through their daughters shared sport and became fast friends. Both girls were the same age, incredibly talented and extremely competitive. My friend acknowledges it was an odd match. She is an IT guru who lives like she works, thoughtful, methodical, no drama. Between job and family, she had little time to make friends. The new woman was intense. A textbook sports mom who never lacked an opinion about anyone except her own daughter. My friend admits she overlooked the warning signs because she was lonely and craved companionship. The first few years the two women bonded during long hours watching their girls practice and time spent traveling to tournaments. They stayed at the same hotels, ate meals together, killed time shopping and gossiped over a hundred cups of coffee. Through their daughters' pre-teen years there was an easy ebb and flow; it did not matter who won or lost, both girls were celebrated and supported.

Years went by, and their friendship began to extend beyond their daughters' sport. One woman called the shots: the other agreed. It was no surprise who was who. My friend, an executive who runs a large company was grateful to just follow instead of lead. They became confidants, spoke almost every day, and enjoyed occasional evenings out with their husbands. When the girls turned 15, balance began to shift and cracks started to form. My friend's daughter excelled beyond her teammates, including her best friend's daughter. The easy ebb and flow of competition, win or lose, was gone. My friend walked around on eggshells, afraid to say too much or too little. Phone calls would go to voicemail. Scheduled get togethers were suddenly cancelled; something came up. Instead of celebrating the hard-earned success, the 'best friend' started to nit-pick everything my friend and her daughter did. Sports talk was off limits. Text messages sat unanswered for hours, then days. The friendship could have died naturally, but mean girls must always stab you in the back on the way out. The explosion came the day before my friend's daughter signed her Division 1 letter of intent to compete at her dream college. The invitation turned out to be the breaking point. When my friend answered her phone the evening before the signing, the insults were personal and meant to cut deep. Her secrets, moments of insecurity and weakness were hurled back at her. It was made clear that they were not friends anymore. Eventually the whispers would get back to my friend, her 'old friend' had betrayed her to anyone who would listen. They never spoke again, the price of ending a relationship with a mean girl is steep.

Jealousy and envy get the best of many women, whether you are 15 or 55. We need to learn to be happy for other women, to help them up and hold them up. By lifting others up, we lift ourselves. Without meaningful female relationships, it is too easy to become lonely and isolated. What a terrible end to a long friendship; what a horrible example shown to both daughters. Women must be big enough and kind enough to be happy when other women (young and old) have successes. The tent is big enough for all of us.

It is difficult to talk about a broken relationship with another woman. Whether it happens in your career or with a girlfriend, it hurts. Girl code tells us that we should have lots of lifelong girlfriends, but nothing is ever that cut and dried. As we get older and life becomes more complicated, we are faced with new responsibilities, challenges, family issues, financial concerns, stress, and sometimes illness. We all experience seasons when we are not at our best. Women never take enough time to process their emotions, deal with issues, and heal; instead, we search for plugs and quick fixes to stop the leak. Why?

We are too busy taking care of everyone else to put ourselves first. When you are not at your best, seek out trusted friends and mentors – women who will surround and protect you during your lonely hours.

Chapter 5
Pulling Up the Ladder

"If you get to the top of the
ladder first, reach down and
offer your hand."

We make a huge misstep when we pull the ladder up after reaching the top. Never forget the hard work that went into achieving your goals. Reach out to the women battling behind you and pull them up too. Make the time to offer guidance and be wise enough to accept it. You may reach the top of many ladders during your journey. Every time you start a new adventure, aim for the top and when you get there, look around and see what you can do next. More importantly, see who you can help next. Be solid in your sense of self and invite other women to sit at your table. Do not be afraid to reach down and help another woman up.

In the 2004 movie *Mean Girls*, a clique called the "Plastics" rule over North Shore High School, Regina George, played by Rachel McAdams, is the queen of the campus mean girl clique. Beautiful, popular, and rich, Regina never misses a chance to belittle her best friends, Karen and Gretchen. Regina delights in bossing them around, insulting them, and playing one against the other. Popularity, power, and plotting are her priorities. Regina graduated from the playground to the halls of North Shore High School with her methods and maneuvers finely tuned. We all know a woman like Regina who does not hesitate to bully and embarrass her friends. A woman who makes no effort to be discreet about her slights. Someone whose friends seem like the oddest choices. They are people she never had anything nice to say about until they were the only ones she had left. Like Regina, she thrives on the power dynamic. She is doing you a favor when she selects you; be grateful. Regina George constantly reminds her besties that everything will be fine as long as they follow her rules, take criticism like a dutiful lieutenant, and snap to attention when she texts. She will never reach down to pull you up.

Being ambitious and hard-driving does not make you a mean girl. You can be intense; you can be intimidating. Those are labels others put on you because of their own insecurity. Mean girls are different, they have malicious intent. They have one goal: get to the top of the ladder first and quickly pull it up. They will let you hang on to their ladder, but they will never offer to help you up. The end of every friendship hurts, some much more than others. Friends bring value to your life, a shoulder to cry on, a champion to cheer you on. Most friendships that end do so naturally; we move away, grow apart, family and work demands tug us in different directions. Life moves on and sometimes friendships do not. Healthy friendships end and life moves on without blame, accusations or threats – no drama. Nothing can prepare you for the end of a friendship with a mean girl. Mean girls cannot walk away; they must burn the place down. It can be a personal friendship, a business partnership, a boss, or coworker. It has been one of the hardest things for me to discuss. Women have such a hard time admitting they were betrayed; they are embarrassed, hurt, and bewildered. I did a little social media test. I often post about women supporting women, positive messages that are a bit introspective. Women respond to encouraging messages, but what if I go edgy? I posted the following question:

> Have you ever had a friend turn their back on you, ghost you, betray you? I have. Women must be kinder to each other.

Crickets, No one likes to admit it, but I want to be a woman who is empowered by acknowledging the good and the disappointing. It is the only way to be a better role model. The post limped along. Was there a lesson in there? I followed it up a few days later with a comfortable post, sitting at my kitchen counter, contemplating my "what's next." The post started an engaging conversation. Things were back to normal. Had I been too edgy, or had I cut too close? No, I thought, women do not like to admit publicly (or maybe at all) that another woman, especially someone who had been a friend, could be so cruel.

I decided to call a few of the women I most admired. Women who constantly volunteer, support charitable organizations, have professional successes – five lunches, five dynamic, attractive, large personality women, five women I respect. After catching up, I admitted that my lunch invitation had a purpose. I asked the question I had posed on social media. Not knowing what to expect, they appeared relieved that someone had finally asked. At first each woman looked away as if to gather their thoughts. Their smile lines tightened, and they shifted uncomfortably. The lost relationships were all unique and ended for different reasons, but the sting was identical.

Each woman used the same words; I knew them by heart. Embarrassed, shocked, lied to, manipulated, avoided and rejected. Two of the women had been bullied by female co-workers, one woman lost a lucrative regional sales job because her female sales manager saw her ambition as a threat. One lost a decades old friendship after a 'new gal' moved to town and turned her best friend against her. One woman shared how she was forced to quit a 15-year career because a rumor had gotten to the corporate office that she was planning to start her own company and take customers with her. The source of the false rumor was a female co-worker. Sabotage, false rumors, jealousy, cruel gossip; all five women had fallen victim to a mean girl. Looking at them, listening to them, knowing them; it was surreal. Five accomplished women, each sharing the blow to their confidence and moments of self-doubt that still hibernate in the back of their minds. Each woman trying to figure out why. For most, the toxic relationship had happened in the workplace and negatively affected their careers.

I shared my own experiences, there is something powerful in being real, being humble, admitting profound disappointment. Like these women, I had learned many lessons the hard way along my own journey. A mentor would have saved me much heartache. Five lunches with five impressive women, an opportunity for me to step up and support other women and receive support in return.

Mentoring has taught me to sit back and listen. Watching good bosses and bad, experiencing valued friendships and toxic ones, changed how I viewed my own journey and more importantly helped me be the kind of leader I wanted to be. Ambitious, tough, successful women do not scare me, but mean women do. The two are night and day. True leaders can reflect on their own actions; the sad truth for mean girls is they are not capable of critiquing themselves. It is their own insecurity and inability to be honest with the one person that matters – themselves. Yes, they do tremendous damage to others, but eventually they find themselves all alone with no true friends. Maybe that was always their goal.

I started mentoring quite accidentally as a young professional in my mid-30s. I did not know I was mentoring; I do not think I realized what a mentor was. During my four years at a women's college, I called it friendship, admiration, respect. As a college freshman and sophomore, I looked up to the women leaders on campus and tried to copy the ones I most admired (copy the best and learn from the worst). As a junior and senior, I was excited to be a leader but never connected that I was now the one setting an example. I liked to talk, and I liked to give advice. What people responded to was how comfortable I was sharing my missteps, even my failures. That came naturally to me, it always has. I understood, without ever being told, that the willingness to be honest and real created trust. As a young professional woman, I was just trying to get to work on time, raise a small child, be a good wife. I did not avail myself of women's groups, especially professional groups, because I did not grasp how important it was to make time for myself and my own development. Some of the professional mistakes I made could have been teachable moments if I had only had a trusted mentor.

When I graduated from Randolph-Macon Woman's College, I was ready to take on the world. My English major had nothing to do with where I ultimately saw my future; they said pick a major and I picked. English was easy for me; I loved to read and write but I always saw my future doing something more exciting, more social. By junior year I knew I was headed for the hospitality industry. I pictured fabulous resorts in exotic locations, traveling the world, maybe the chance to work abroad. I had never been out of the country except a high school bus trip to Montreal, Canada with the French club. I had only been on a plane twice, both puddle jumpers from one state to the next. My parents made it clear that having a "good" job lined up by graduation was a requirement, not an option. No one had even heard of a gap year or taking time to find your passion. My mom and dad would have flipped. So instead of traveling the world, I headed to Dayton, Ohio as a management trainee at Stouffer's Dayton Plaza Hotel, no beach, no palm trees, no Mai Tai's.

It never dawned on me to consider the culture shock of leaving a small women's college and stepping into a completely male dominated industry. The decision would set the stage for some of my worst missteps. Most of them were with other women managers. I wish I had been afforded more opportunity, especially as a young manager, to work with and for women. There were very few women in hotel food and beverage when I started my career. Slowly, more women joined the industry, but it took many years and many slip-ups before I learned to work effectively with women in the workplace who were above or below my position. I made the error of viewing women as being potential girlfriends, something I never did with my male peers. I judged the women thumbs up or thumbs down, in or out. Women are always looking to find new friends; we are social by nature, and I think that in part causes us problems in the workplace.

I share an example I am not proud of. It happened when I was working at a hotel in Anchorage, Alaska. My husband had received an assignment to Elmendorf Air Force Base, so I left Stouffer's after a decade and made the move, with our first child, from California to Alaska. I started at the Anchorage hotel as a catering manager and was quickly promoted to catering director. After a year I was promoted to food and beverage director, the first female to have the job. The same day my male boss announced to the whole staff that a woman from outside the hotel had been hired to fill my former position. The outgoing male food and beverage director had been tasked by the male general manager with hiring one of my key team members. Why? I was mortified by what I perceived to be their total lack of confidence in my ability. What message did this send to the managers (all male) who were now reporting to me? That a woman cannot be entrusted with such an important decision. Did I sit down and discuss the slight with my boss? Share how I felt? No, I had received a big promotion and was afraid to make waves. What was done was done, or so I thought.

On the way out the door the former food and beverage director dropped the new gal's resume on my desk. Seriously? Zero hospitality experience? Whose daughter, niece, or best friend, was she? Her first day was our first introduction. As soon as I met her, I knew why he had hired her. She was gorgeous, high heels, impeccable makeup and a bright floral dress. Remember this is Alaska, bright floral dresses are truly statement making. We were oil and vinegar. I started judging her immediately. I could not get past feeling undercut (and jealous) and so I took out my misplaced irritation on her. I gave her zero guidance – cutting off my nose to spite my face – because I wanted her to fail. I wish I had had a mentor; they could have saved me from being a total jerk.

My boss, general manager of the hotel, was in his late 60s, short, portly, round tortoise shell glasses and a full head of perfectly coiffed gray hair. He was a very kind man but had no interest in mentoring his managers. He expected everyone to just do their job. The struggle between my catering manager and me was too much for him to handle. I put him in an awful position by constantly complaining about her. Finally, the three of us sat down to air our grievances. He had not set expectations for the meeting; he just wanted us to be friends. The meeting only made things worse. He treated us differently because we were 'young' women (33ish). He talked about his three daughters and their struggles at times to get along. He gave us fatherly advice when he should have been speaking as our boss with the expectations of the company. At one point he chided us, "You are the same age; you both have young children; work at the same hotel; you should be best friends." Of course we should! How silly of us. The meeting accomplished nothing; we both left frustrated.

Two days later my boss came into my office and announced that HR was hiring a professional counselor to help "you girls" resolve your differences. How condescending. Did I push back? No. Once again I shoveled my irritation on to the pile in the back of my brain. I knew better. This was not a girl problem; it was my problem. I had gotten to the top of the ladder and refused to pull her up with me because she was not my choice. That is hard to admit, even after all these years. I purposely refused to give her the guidance and training she needed and deserved. The constant aggravation was exhausting me. There was no excuse for not dealing honestly with my boss in the beginning. I had allowed the situation to spin out of control. A counseling session would just add to my humiliation.

I invited her to lunch off property. I apologized and took responsibility. If we could not work this out, one of us was going to end up losing our job. I assured her that I was at risk too. I explained why I resented the way she was hired; I wanted her to understand my misplaced resentment. Then I told her I would do whatever I could to fix our professional relationship. We did not need to be friends, but we needed to be successful together. Foolishly, I had refused to see the part I played until it was too late. I had discounted her from day one because she was someone else's choice, not mine. We both could have been so successful if I had taken a different approach. But I chose to be jealous and resentful. There was no happy ending. She and I worked together for a few more months. I am guessing she started looking for a new job the day after our lunch.

Yes, I hired a woman to replace her. I had much to prove to myself. The new manager was successful in large part because she had a boss who was also her mentor. When I moved on, she was promoted to replace me. It is as important to offer help as it is to accept it. Being the boss comes with added responsibilities, both in managing up and down. I had reached the top of the ladder and missed an incredible opportunity to lift another woman up with me.

Learn to seek out trusted colleagues and join professional organizations. Surround yourself with people who will give you honest counsel so that you can do and be your best. You will not fear supporting other women if you are confident in yourself. When you get to the top of your ladder, breathe. It is the beginning of the work, not the end. You may reach the top of several ladders over your life. Ladders are everywhere you choose to excel, philanthropies, career, social groups, volunteer organizations, elected positions. Remember that more is expected of you when you reach the top, and those looking up will be judging you accordingly.

As I learned to work well with women, I found I worked better with men as well. I stopped looking at every woman as a potential girlfriend. Whatever the project, challenge, or task, I started judging women by what I could learn from them. It takes effort to figure people out and admit that you need to try a new approach. Do not get stuck on getting your way. You must be willing to consider that you are the one who needs to do things differently. A gal I know well yelled my name across our local grocery store parking lot. This woman is quite the character; let me leave it at that. She is one of those women that is always offended by something – today it was the men in her office. She had been with the same company for years; she knew her stuff and was a workhorse, but when the management team gathered for strategy sessions, as the only female, she said her opinions and ideas were disregarded. When I asked her how she responded to the 'slight,' she said she pushed harder until she just gave up. Well, if I saw the pattern, I am sure everyone at that table saw it. So, what do you do when you have earned your spot at the table, but your opinion is always side-stepped? You change your strategy and mix things up.

I shared a story with her about a boss I worked for when I was in my late 20s. He was early 40s, married with two children. He was on the fast track. The first day I met him he told me the hotel business was no place for women and went about trying to convince me that I needed to pursue a different career by disregarding every idea I had. One day in a rather heated management meeting, and me being a young woman who would not back down, he looked me right in the eye and said, "You are too emotional, too unreasonable, you sound just like one of my kids." Ahh, we had gotten to the real issue. It changed everything. I tried a new tactic and started pushing smarter. It worked. I realized that his perception of me, right or wrong, affected how he dealt with me. Of course, his comment was sexist, thank heavens the workplace has matured since then, but the point is that I needed to take more responsibility for what I was putting out there.

I asked this woman if she had ever considered a new tactic. She pushed back. Why should she be the one who must change? I assured her that a slight change in approach is not selling your soul. What, I asked, if you did more homework before the meetings and went in with a strategy that anticipated what you knew was coming? Have a historical list of past projects that did not work out as well as planned, projects where your input was sidelined. As you present your ideas, refer back in a way that is not about winning but rather about making the best management decision for the company. Being a 'bull in the china shop,' as I learned long ago, costs you, not anyone else. Today she runs the company, I am willing to bet that she continues to mix things up.

Many women are territorial; it is the clique mentality. It goes back to the playground and that unwritten rule that women seem to have that nobody should upset the group dynamic; no one should change the rules. We learn at a very young age that being surrounded provides protection. We naturally stress out over the risk of losing all we have accomplished. Pulling up the ladder becomes an automatic response after years of fighting to get to the top. Do not be intimidated by younger ambitious women; you were once them. Be their mentor and show them how much hard work went into earning all you have accomplished. Do not forget how resilient your own journey has made you. Too many young women, especially those who do not have the benefit of guidance, think things look easier than they are. When faced with adversity they fold because they do not know how to manage through adversity. Those who are given too much without earning it take success for granted.

High achieving women tend to make things look easy and are hesitant to share struggles. Surround yourself with women who bring value to your life. We are all busy, all working to get somewhere, so do not waste time on friends who do not bring you joy. Too many women do not support other women. Choose friends who will applaud your successes and hold you close when you have losses, and when you get to the top of the ladder first, offer your hand.

Chapter 6
Win with Class,
Lose with Grace

"Be careful what you accept in other people's behavior because you will be judged by the actions of those you embrace. Who you choose to surround yourself with speaks as much about who you are as it does about them."

Work harder, listen more intently, and respect others time and counsel. There are too many voices in our ears telling us that we are special. Nice thought, but not reality. We are being fed the false narrative that our feelings – our truth – is all that matter. We lose friends, colleagues, and even family relationships over this kind of thinking. Sorry, but there is a big world out there full of people who could care less how hard you pound your fist. Save your energy; use it for change. Own your individuality, but also be self-aware. Be willing to be critical of yourself, and do not hesitate to analyze how you think, act, and treat others. Self-love is great, but without some introspection, it can be harmful. I choose self-value over self-love. No one is responsible for my happiness besides me, so it is important that I try to put myself in situations where the odds are on my side. If I make a mistake, I move on. Win or lose, I will still be the best version of me. Care about yourself but be realistic. Do not expect others to care about you in the same all-encompassing way.

A successful life means putting yourself out there in positions that are not your first choice. We have all suffered through meetings, events, luncheons, dinners, and a variety of social and professional obligations. We attend for personal or professional gain, to network and form new connections. It is an investment that is necessary to get us where we ultimately want to be. It is vital to your success to sample different experiences. Just be realistic, not every group is a fit and some are downright duds. Value yourself and choose to put yourself in settings and around people who fill you up. Be okay with saying no to groups or causes that do not. It has taken me a long time to learn to be selective. Selective is an empowering word. Lessons learned, good or bad, over the years, help you choose where you want to invest your time. Try new things and be okay with moving on if they do not work out. You will still have slipups, but they will become more tolerable and less frequent because you are more selective.

I attended a seminar marketed for women entrepreneurs. The marketing materials promised an afternoon full of insight, education, and inspiration. The keynote speaker was an accomplished business woman and author. I was writing my first book at the time, <u>Walking in my Shoes, A Woman's Story of Leadership</u>. The event seemed the perfect opportunity for me to get a dose of inspiration as I wrestled with my last few chapters. The hotel ballroom was packed; you could feel the energy. I had never heard the keynote speaker, but I had already formed a positive opinion based on her professional photo and impressive resume. Gorgeous, mid 50s, perfectly put together – the black suit, the heels, the hair, the makeup, the smile. A good reminder that we judge first by what we see.

I sat with 200 other professional women; these were my people. When the lights dimmed, I settled back, breathed in, and slowly breathed out. I was in my mental and physical ready-set-learn position. Blaring music jarred me out of my mental Zen, laser lights danced across the ballroom. The speaker bopped out on stage, clapping and shimmying from side to side. "Come on ladies, out of your seats, show me what you've got." I had never heard the song and judging from the murmuring in the audience, I was not the only one. I admit I felt weird. I chalked it up to some new motivational thing. I am not a dance around the room kind of gal. It never got better for me. After gobs of self-love talk, we were asked to gather all our things and switch seats. There was a reason I chose the back row; I stood up, pretended to move and sat down again in the same place. Finally, all 200 women were settled, you can imagine the commotion; the Zen was gone. The speaker had more fun planned, she asked us to introduce ourselves to the women on either side of us and give them a compliment. The compliment naturally went directly to physical appearance, smile, outfit, shoes, so cliché. I complimented my 'neighbors' for making the time to do something nice for themselves by attending the event; they complimented my suit. I was literally looking to make a mad dash to the lady's room to hide until the lovefest was over. I found myself obsessing over what game she would ask us to play next, to the point that I missed half the value in her speech.

I had not done my homework; I do not think I was the only one. The speaker had a YouTube channel I could have watched. She had a social media presence I could have searched. I ordered her book but had not read it yet. I did not take the time because I was busy with other things and made my choice to buy a ticket based on a glance at a marketing piece. It was obviously not the right motivational style for me. What a great reminder! Just because we are all women does not mean that we think the same way, learn the same way, or get inspired by the same things. I have always felt that the whole woman-kum-baya thing was forced on us solely because of our sex. Our tank gets filled up in very different ways, so take a moment and reflect on the experiences that left you feeling ready to take on the world. That is where you want to put yourself. I came back to the office feeling like I had just been to the therapist. Lesson learned; we are all motivated differently and it is up to us to know what works.

Another lesson I learned the hard way was that you cannot assume that everyone who asks for your guidance really wants it. Sometimes you feel an obligation because the request is coming from a colleague who you feel duty-bound to help. Do not let yourself be taken advantage of; learn to say no to unproductive relationships. It is not selfish to have boundaries. Your time is a gift so do not give it to someone who demands it or wastes it. As I have had the opportunity to mentor women, I have come to see that, even in mentoring, different styles do not always make for a perfect fit. After some unproductive time and effort, I now know I am better at dealing with crisis situations or long-term strategic planning and goal setting. Be realistic; being asked for advice and having that advice taken are two different things. My ego has gotten me into some very aggravating situations when the person who asked for my advice and guidance, went and did the exact opposite. Yes, I took it personally.

Not everyone in a position of leadership respects another leader's time. Some develop the bad habit of advice shopping. This is true in business and public service. We have all experienced the frustration of giving hours to someone who implored you to advise them and connect them with others in your circle. You fall for it, you help them put together a plan of action, they walk away grateful and seemingly empowered, and then they completely flip. It turns out that their style of decision making is to shop around until they find someone who tells them what they want to hear. What they are telling you is that your time has no value because they would rather browse than buy. They may be in a leadership position, but that does not make them a leader. Like an exhausting friend, this person becomes an exhausting colleague who potential mentors start to dodge. Their weakness is an inability to stand up for anything or speak with conviction. They are exhausting. There is no helping a person like this, and do not permit them into your inner circle. Sometimes you must walk away; not all mentor relationships click.

It becomes difficult when you are continually asked for your time and counsel by a colleague who has a proven track record of not valuing your advice. What do you do when that colleague pleads for help but is determined to jump into shark-infested waters? One of the most frustrating experiences I ever had in my professional capacity was with a woman who was on a mission to self-destruct and pull everyone down with her. When she called, asking for my guidance, I fell for it. My ego fooled me into believing that she respected my position and wanted my counsel to get out of the mess; certainly, this time she would listen. But I was nothing more than another pawn on her long, albeit impressive, list. She went from one professional woman to the next begging for their help, stating her admiration. Blah, blah, blah. When our advice was not what she wanted to hear, she moved on to her next pawn. As one 'would-be' mentor stated, "I just gave her two hours of my life that I will never get back, and for what? Leadership is no place for a woman like her. She is incapable of making tough decisions when it really counts."

She was a woman who shed tears rather than show resolve. As a woman in a position of leadership, I find the crying game insincere. We need to toughen up. Too many women make the mistake of using tears to elicit sympathy, to buy time; poor me. I had to accept that she wanted pity, not accountability. I was watching a woman, in a position of responsibility, walk the plank. Should I have cared? Yes, if you believe in mentoring, accept that sometimes it will be draining. Would I do it again in this case? No. Did this end in disaster? Yes.

There is no getting around the fact that leadership entails responsibilities. If you want the title but not the responsibility, own it and accept that your best job is being a good lieutenant. Regrettably, not everyone who ends up in leadership is a leader. We all know them. We have worked for them, served on committees and volunteered with them. Many of them get by until the dreaded day comes when their leadership is needed. Most failed leaders I have known never saw the problem coming because they are not strategic thinkers. They are in it for the wrong reasons.

There is no girl code that demands women support each other just because we are the same sex. Will you get along with every woman you work with, volunteer with or serve with? No, and that is okay. I do not like every man I meet, but there seems to be a presumption that women should automatically like each other. Women are not mean girls because they do not like every woman they are introduced to. We have all been in professional and social situations where we respectfully worked with women with whom we did not care to have any other relationship. It is simply the choice we make to include some women in our lives beyond social niceties. The same holds up for mentoring; not every woman will be a perfect fit. Finding a trusted mentor is very much like developing a valued friendship, some relationships get to that level, most do not.

As a woman in elected office, it was often presumed that I would always side with a woman over a man. No, I will not support based on sex but rather on substance. I received a very angry email from a college student after a heated local election. While I appreciated her defense of her candidate, two sentences stood out: "You had an obligation as a woman to support another woman. I have zero respect for you because you do not understand that women must always support women against men." Against? There are too many women who fall for that thinking, but what has surprised me most is the number of male colleagues who assume that because of my sex, I naturally side with a woman over a man regardless of merit.

A very good friend called me to invite me for coffee; I was mayor at the time, and she wanted me to meet an 'amazing woman' who had just moved to town. My friend was almost too joyful about this new gal who "is so excited to get to know everyone because she plans on being super involved in the community." Hmmm, I know better. I begged off coffee but promised to make sure I met this new 'super gal'. I was bound to run into her if, as promised, she jumped right in. Within a few weeks, her name was floating around town, as were her posts. It quickly became obvious that getting involved meant causing commotion. I was reminded of a wind-up doll; just wind her up and point her in the wrong direction. I never did meet her and would not know her if she walked up to me, but I sure know what she thought of me (yup, nothing good). Lots of opinions for a new girl. You would think she had lived in our town for decades and would have done everything differently and better. A living, breathing mean girl, desperate to be accepted no matter what the cost. Then one day, she was gone. On to conquer a new community. I am sure she will set them straight.

It is no different than the girls on the playground who are willing to be mean to other girls to earn a coveted spot in the fort. This woman got showered with attention and welcomed with open arms because she was willing to do anything for admission. There will always be the used and the users. Fortunately, my girlfriend saw the red flags and did a U-turn; most women did. It was predictable to watch those who chose to embrace her viciousness by liking her posts and egging her on. Be careful what you accept in other people's behavior because you will be judged by the actions of those you embrace. Who you choose to surround yourself with speaks as much about who you are as it does about them.

I knew a woman for many years, someone I would consider a friendly acquaintance. I watched her fall prey to a mean girl. But as often happens, she could not see what everyone else could see. Users target our desire to belong, to be in the mix, and to be supported. For mean girls, using the people around them is the only way they know how to have relationships. Understand that you will always be supporting their efforts, not the other way around. They feel entitled because they consider themselves better than the worker bees that they surround themselves with. If your phone only rings when they need something, be a realist. Incessant users are masters at making you feel like they really care about you. It is the only currency they have. Do not fall for it, promises will never be kept.

Sometimes the price of admission is being silent when a friend is being hurt, disparaged, or gossiped about. Choosing to get caught up with people who demand this kind of loyalty is dangerous. You approve of their methods by staying silent and going along with them. Be cautious if the price of acceptance includes turning on old friends. Be mindful of how your new friends treat other people because, ultimately, they will treat you the same way when they no longer need you. Who you surround yourself with can negatively affect other friendships, acquaintances, potential clients, and opportunities and you will never know it. People are judging you all the time. They are judging you by the behavior with which you are aligning yourself.

Chapter 7
Have Enough Pride in
Yourself to be Decent

"Too often we learn as little girls
that the measure of our success is
popularity rather than being okay
with our uniqueness."

I never imagined I would live in the same house, in the same town, for 27 years and counting. When your childhood is spent constantly moving, there is never time to grow roots or feel like you belong. All I remember is packing, unpacking, and feeling alone. Finally making friends, only to be the new kid again over and over. As a child I lived in Maryland (twice), Connecticut, West Virginia, and Pennsylvania (twice). My friendship foundation was wobbly at best. I regret that growing up I did not live anywhere long enough to make strong connections, ones that would last a lifetime. Those early friendships are so important because they teach you how to be a true friend, to weather disappointments, keep secrets, share feelings, welcome new friends into your group, and learn how much it hurts when you lose a good friend.

The summer between my sophomore and junior years in high school I worked at the local mall. Didn't we all? I manned the candy counter at Bowman's Department Store. A week into summer break, a new girl was hired part-time. She was assigned to the women's clothing department, which was right across the aisle from the candy counter. I could spot a new kid a mile away. Her family had just moved to town, and she would be in my class at Cumberland Valley High School. She and I became fast friends. We spent every lunch break together, cruising the mall and flirting with the boys who worked the counter at Orange Julius. We chatted endlessly when the store manager was not around. Pretty unprofessional now that I know better, but she would stand at the edge of her department, I would stand at the end of the candy counter, and we would chit chat across the aisle just nodding at the shoppers who 'interrupted' as they walked between us. We never ran out of things to chatter about.

On our days off we met at the local pool, a favorite teen hangout. The cool spot was a grassy mound behind the pool deck, where all the parents with little kids sat. We always made sure our towels were right next to each other's. I introduced her to everyone from school; she was cool, and I felt special that we were friends. The summer before, I had been the new girl; it had been a lonely summer and an intimidating first day of tenth grade, not knowing a soul. My new friend would have a great first day; I would make sure of it. But sadly, summer friendships are sometimes just that. As I reminisce through that summer, I realize my memories are so clear because of the hurt that came after school started in the fall.

For three months we were inseparable, but the start of school triggered an invisible reset button that I did not know existed. She moved on without me. She was welcomed into the popular group, but that did not include me. My place in the high school student hierarchy was already cast in stone. She would soon have a new best friend. It is bizarre that so many years later, one friendship would stick with me like it has. I feel strangely transported back in time, reliving the heartbreak of losing my friend. Monumental for the 16-year-old me. Friendships do not always last and while it can be very painful, we need to experience disappointment when we are young so we are wiser when we are older.

My summertime bestie was a really nice girl. Our friendship ended because bigger things around us dictated it. Ultimately, we were forced apart because our friend groups did not mix – the law according to high school. One friend becomes popular; one does not. One goes through gawky years, the other blossoms like a rose. One gets invited, and one gets left out. With time, we realize that we must work hard to maintain the friendships that matter to us, but sometimes even effort is not enough. Learning from hurt, getting our feelings crushed when we are young makes us more empathetic adults, parents, partners, and friends. The mentors our daughters need.

Women need close girlfriends, so be selfish and guard the women in your inner circle. Of course, you cannot be friends, much less close friends, with every woman you meet. Age, interests, children, family, business, and daily responsibilities dictate where we investment our time, and friendship is an investment. Have a special spot saved for the women you connect with when the timing is not perfect; in the future, it may be. Have multiple circles of women in your life; make space. By allowing friendships to ebb and flow in and out of your circles, you save a place for them. Friendships should not be easily discarded, and the chance to connect with someone special should be considered a gift. The 16-year-old me did not understand that, and neither did my summertime friend. It was all or nothing; those were the rules in high school. She had to choose, and she chose the popular girls.

We all know women who still carry around that high school rulebook. Most of us have unknowingly befriended a woman like this; we have the battle scars to prove it. There is no piggy bank where they saved up all the meaningful moments, memories, kindnesses, and trust. Why save something you never saw value in? For them, life is all about today. We must teach our daughters to make more space, value close female friendships, and not be careless with another woman's trust. Yes, we want to raise independent young women who are not afraid to stand up for themselves, but that does not excuse a lack of common decency.

I do not use the word friend casually. I am a woman who has a few very close friends and a huge circle of friendly acquaintances. Honestly, I like to be alone. I do not enjoy talking things out; I am happier mulling things over in my own head. Eating lunch alone or sitting in a coffee shop by myself makes me happy. No style is right or wrong, but close friends 'match up.' I am a friend better suited for women who are confident and low maintenance. Now if you need me, I will drop what I am doing to help you. Calling or texting just for the heck of it? Nope. I will never be late, and if I say I am going to do something, I will. Ask for my opinion, you will get it with absolute honesty.

During my teen years, I wished like many of us that I could be one of the popular girls. They always seemed to be having fun, sleepovers, pizza parties, dates. I daydreamed about being in their secret society; at least that is what I imagined it was like. But it was never going to be. We moved too much; I had skinny legs and knobby knees, wore braces, a retainer and had a face covered in freckles. I went on four dates in high school that I can recall. Homecoming twice, Prom once and the opening night of Jaws at our local movie theatre. It was not until I went to college that I had the chance to stay put long enough to figure the whole friendship thing out.

I went from a huge high school in blue collar Mechanicsburg, Pennsylvania, to a small, preppy women's college in Lynchburg, Virginia. The college no longer exists as I knew it. In 2007, Randolph-Macon Woman's College became a coed college and was renamed – the only way for it to survive financially. I ended up there quite accidentally. In high school, I babysat for neighbors; the woman had graduated from R-MWC in the 1960s. She kept her college yearbooks on the shelf in the family room, and I loved looking at them. The girls were dressed in preppy Dean sweaters and penny loafers. They looked so self-assured and sophisticated, ready to take on the world. I daydreamed through those pages. I adored the crisp white button-down shirts and tasteful jewelry. I wanted to be one of those young women sharing campus life with other confident women. It sounds silly to say it now, but I believed that I would have a better chance of making friends at an all-women's college. Percentages were on my side!

I was attracted to the intimacy of the small college campus and loved the feeling of belonging to a tight knit community. There was a great social dynamic on campus. Those first few months of freshman year were all about figuring it out. Nothing worked out the way I had imagined. I was enamored with the upper-class women who were active in campus organizations; they seemed so comfortable in their own skin. I decided to focus on organizations and clubs that interested me and I stopped being so preoccupied with searching for friendships. Too often we learn as little girls that the measure of our success is popularity rather than being okay with our uniqueness. I finally found where I fit, what my talents were. We miss opportunities (and waste valuable time) worrying about things that ultimately do not matter, wanting to be someone we will never be. Finding our place is where we will find meaningful friendships.

Looking back, making friends cannot be forced. It is as much about the right people connecting with you as it is about you connecting with them. As I became more mature, and a little more confident in my own skin, I became better friend material. Age fixed many things that I longed for when I was younger. You must find the right place, and then quite naturally, you will find the right people. Commonality provides a foundation for friendship to grow. What kind of friendship you have depends on how much you are both willing to give and receive and if the timing is right. As mothers, grandmothers, aunts, friends, co-workers, and mentors, it is such an important conversation to have with the young women in our lives.

I miss the days when we did not talk about money, religion, or politics; now it is all we talk about. People are obsessed with pronouncing their opinions, regardless of the effect on friendships they claim to value. No matter your party affiliation or how you are aligned on issues, the playing field has become so aggressive, filled with half-truths, anger, and ugliness. We cannot have any kind of conversation about friendship, or even about women supporting each other, without acknowledging the damage politics has done at every level.

Too many female friendships have fallen victim to politics. I ran into one of these victims at our Tom Thumb grocery store a year ago. I had not seen this woman since COVID-19. After a hug and all the normal niceties, I asked how her best friend was. It was her best friend who introduced us many years ago. When you saw one, you always saw the other. They were neighbors, both athletic and played the same sport. Their children were the same age, and the two families often vacationed together. I felt like I knew them better than I actually did, just based on all the pictures they posted over the years. The moment her best friend's name came out of my mouth; I knew I had made a gaffe. Her response was quick and curt: "I have no idea how she is; we haven't spoken since 2020." It was a declaration more than an answer. Okay, I thought, how odd. But I pressed forward, "I am sorry if I am being nosey but what happened in 2020?" All I could think of was COVID-19. Oh, heavens, had something terrible happened to one of their families? I swear she glared at me as though it were preposterous that I did not know, but then like lightning it hit me, it was not COVID-19, it was the presidential election. I felt so awkward that all I could get out of my mouth was a throaty moan. That was the end of our pickle aisle reunion; we gave each other an uncomfortable hug and scurried off in opposite directions. Their friendship had stood the test of time; until politics put up a roadblock. I do not take anything away from women who are standing up for a cause and fighting for their beliefs. I just wonder; is there a point when we have given too much?

When I finished my second term as mayor, I could not run again due to term limits (which I love). I was excited to move on, but it was tougher than I thought it would be. For 14 years, I had been in public office. My identity had become entwined with my public persona. Ironically, 15 years earlier, I had run for office because I felt a calling toward mentoring young people and believed elected office would give me a platform to get meaningful things accomplished. As a woman mayor, I took advantage of the opportunity I had been given to mentor young women. I spent hundreds of hours speaking to student groups, community organizations, and women's clubs. I hosted numerous events to support our small businesses, particularly those owned by women. Public office will wear anyone down, especially in the current political climate, but with a pandemic, economic uncertainty and the death of staff members, friends, and relatives, you find yourself scared and uncertain. Yes, I was frightened for my community, our residents, staff, and businesses. It is easy to second-guess now that we are back to near normal, but in March and April of 2020, it felt like the locusts were coming. You could not see them or hear them; you did not know how many would swarm over your community, but they were coming; it was terrifying to feel so responsible yet so helpless.

In May 2021, I left a much different community than the one I ran to serve in 2004 – one wounded by the pandemic, social unrest, and political fury. I felt as if I had been on an incredible journey. So, I did what most people would do – well, not really – I wrote a book. It was supposed to be a fluff book, full of lessons learned during my time as mayor. I quickly realized that what I wanted to write was a book about women in leadership. It had zero to do with politics, thus the title, <u>Walking in my Shoes, A Woman's Story of Leadership.</u> Note: leadership, not politics. But the partisan foolery would follow; no one is immune from mini boycotts! I had an appointment at a local woman owned business. I have been a client since they opened and never miss a chance to support them publicly and through social media. But I discovered that there are women in my own community who would rather hurt a local business than shop at the same place I do. So much for women supporting women-owned businesses. Go figure that one out. The business received a call from a client canceling her appointment. She would not be back! Was it poor service? Was it the price? No, it was me, the ex-mayor. She felt totally justified. If I were a client, someone who had different political views than she did, how could she ever darken the doorstep of this woman's business again? Talk about taking a stand, albeit a wasted one. If this does not remind you of little mean girls on the playground, what does? How ridiculous. She should have picked up the phone and called me since I was her problem. All she did was hurt a woman-owned business and the employees who work there. Just another example of mean girls who do not care who they hurt to make a point. What point? We will never know.

Women often hold other women to unattainable standards. Rarely do we measure men with the same yardstick. It seems so much easier for women to hurt other women. It has nothing to do with disagreeing, it has everything to do with being mean. Do friendships end? Absolutely. Does it have to be horrible? Absolutely not. Do you try to publicly humiliate a former friend or damage their business? Why would you? We need to raise strong girls because girls who grow up lacking self-confidence often become women who strike out at others; they are jealous, unkind, and do not value friendship. They are the mean girls on the playground, all grown up, always looking for someone to injure so they feel better about themselves, temporarily. Women need to cut each other a break. We need women as mentors, sharing their knowledge, being engaged, offering balance, not backstabbing. Nothing gets done when people stay in their corners of the ring and only meet in the center to punch each other out. Have enough pride in yourself to be decent.

Never disregard the hours spent together sharing worries, insecurities, celebrations, victories, every emotion, and every life situation. Whether you are still friends or the friendship is long over be a decent human being. I feel nothing but sympathy for women who cannot respect friendship because they do not know how to be a true friend.

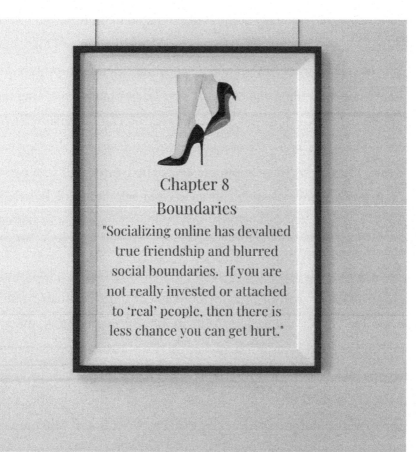

Chapter 8
Boundaries
"Socializing online has devalued
true friendship and blurred
social boundaries. If you are
not really invested or attached
to 'real' people, then there is
less chance you can get hurt."

We have all had to make the decision to walk away, unfollow, unfriend, block, delete, and move on. Everyone does not deserve access to you. Would you walk up to a random person in the grocery store and ask them to look at your family's bikini clad vacation pictures? If you are operating this way online, pull the plug. Be real, social media friends and followers are not your buddies, and I would be willing to bet there are some stalkers mixed in there. I watch some of the women who are always starting the drama online. They have their own little mean girl clique. Opportune friends empowered by shared anger, battling the cause! If you do not have a real friend to pick up the phone and call, do not worry, you can find plenty of fill-ins on social media. I cannot guarantee the quality, but they are easy to find. How many women put the kids to bed, grab a glass or two of pinot, and get busy? Some of these women who fight side by side do not even know each other. If they had to share a cup of coffee, I doubt they would even like each other. They are not fixers or doers; their role (at least as they see it) is to point out other's failings, shortcomings, and mistakes — real or imagined. They can smell a misstep a mile away. The drama gangs are out there in every community and yes, they create good entertainment (cue up the popcorn memes), but we have to take responsibility for our part in feeding the beast by giving them a stage and then grabbing a seat to watch the fireworks. Even when you are not involved, reading angry threads and watching the bullying will affect your spirit. Be bold; leave unhealthy groups and pages. Block, delete, and unfriend the unkindness.

The drama is not victimless; it can do real harm to neighbors, businesses, and community pride. The determination to get likes, comments, and cause arguments becomes addicting to people who are desperate for attention or relevance. These fire starters do not care what your experience is; they only care about their own. What is perplexing is when they start calling other women derogatory, ugly names and then later have the lunacy to refer to them as mean girls. Mirror check. I remember a local restaurant getting bashed on social media by a woman who notoriously starts fires. For five days in a row after her post, I went to the restaurant. I moved all my meetings there. I posted pictures from the restaurant and spent some extra money on food to go. It goes back to the bully on the playground. You must do something! Scrolling by is not good enough. Make a mental note. Do something to offset the damaging post. Too many of us are sitting on the sidelines, not defending good people and businesses. Negative behavior continues if we keep giving it oxygen. Get in your car and patronize the business; if it is a good person being attacked, send them a kind message or text. Use your platform and connections to do good.

I am not a judge or jury when it comes to social media. What I do know is that for too many, it has created an effortless substitute for real friendship, especially for women. It taps into the whole editorial that we are too busy to make time for real people, lunch, coffee, or a walk in the park. We do not even call anymore; we text acronyms and emojis. Posting, sharing, and commenting have allowed people we do not have a relationship with to sit at our dinner table — just to watch. It is a bit creepy if you really think about it. How many people click on your pictures to examine the background? The migration to socializing online has devalued true friendship and blurred social boundaries. If you are not really invested in or attached to 'real' people, then there is less chance you can get hurt. If we constantly criticize other women, businesses, and our community openly on social media, do we expect anyone to think we are good friend material? After watching the fights on social media during the 2020 pandemic, I imagine there are people who never want to be seen in public again without a mask, not for protection but to disguise themselves. Talk about no boundaries.

Pray and forgive. Pray and forgive. Sorry, but sometimes that is a bunch of baloney. I am here to tell you that you do not have to forgive anyone if you do not want to. Take ownership of your boundaries. Decide what you will and will not accept from people. Forgive, forget, and move on if it is the best choice for you; do not feel you have to live by anyone else's golden rules. Honestly, some people do not deserve your forgiveness. Make the decision to walk away, unfollow, unfriend, block, delete, cut all ties and move on. Imagine how peaceful it will be to scroll without seeing their long-winded self-importance. Choose to invest your time and energy in healthy women who treat you and others with respect. My whole outlook on life changed when I realized I could be calm and classy yet still take no sh*t and set solid boundaries. The most important person I need to protect first and foremost is myself. Like the emergency instructions on an airplane, put your oxygen mask on first, then help others.

I wish I had learned how to set better boundaries and recognize impending disaster earlier in life. Today unhealthy relationships are often referred to as toxic. I call it what it is: a disaster waiting to happen. It is an important message we need to share with our daughters. There will always be heartache but there is nothing worse than the betrayal of someone you used to consider a dear friend. Boundaries are a fortress for your heart and soul. Boundaries are a blueprint that guides you to honestly evaluate the relationships you choose. I chose the wrong friend and I paid for it. That was always the way it was going to end. I bet we can all agree on these five truths:

1. We have been backstabbed.

2. We have been left out.

3. We have been gossiped about.

4. We have been posted about.

5. We are responsible to set our own boundaries.

We need to teach our daughters that there will always be a place for the mean girls if as grown women we continue to excuse their behavior. We fear standing up to them because, regardless of age, we all want to be liked, and most of us do not like confrontations. Plus, they can be horribly ugly. Talking about a mean girl we know, a friend said, "I steer clear of her socially; I want her to think I like her so I give her posts a thumbs up. I have to because she keeps track." Keeps track? The internet has emboldened mean girls. They mistake 'likes' for clout, and they are watching to see who agrees. How sad for them. Own your own power and take responsibility for your own behavior. Do not tell yourself that your actions are justified by some greater authority. You speak for no one but yourself.

I settled into my favorite booth in the far corner of the restaurant, looking out at the Main Street station in downtown Grapevine, Texas, the Christmas Capitol of Texas. I have spent untold hours here writing and watching the vintage steam locomotive, the Tarantula train, pull out of the station making the 21-mile trip to the historic Fort Worth Stockyards. I write better surrounded by the past; it seems to center me in the present and challenge me to contemplate a better future. The station now shares the tracks with the less-storied Amtrak that runs from Dallas to Fort Worth, but it keeps the station busy like train stations from a bygone era – the perfect spot to meet two dear friends who I have known for almost 25 years. Two pinots and a Moscow Mule arrived; we raised our glasses and toasted our friendship. Our children are grown; one friend is a grandma times four. We have raised boys and girls, eight children altogether of varying ages.

I treasure the life experiences I have shared with these women. Our friendship has ebbed and flowed naturally as we followed a similar path but faced different challenges over the years. We had grabbed a date on the calendar, a rare day with nowhere to run to next, so we sat for hours laughing, catching up and reminiscing. Spending time with them is always a vitamin shot; I feel energized on the way home.

We met through our neighborhood bunco group. The original group of 12 women (three tables of four) started out playing the dice game bunco once a month as a way to meet the ladies in our new neighborhood. It was a perfect way to get to know each other, talk kids, houses, school, and jobs. Our children were very young, and most attended the same two schools; those were the kid centric years. But the years marched on, neighbors moved, and the dynamic of the group gradually changed. I always looked forward to bunco night and protected its spot on my calendar. It was a night out, a break from the kids, and dad oversaw dinner and homework. Selfishly, I needed a night out. My home life was not great; it had not been for years. I hoped the move to Texas, leaving the military, starting new careers, and building a house would be a fresh start. As a child, moving was always a chance to start over with a clean slate. But the reset only lasted a few years, then the tensions crept back in. We were about three years away from divorcing. No one in the group knew it but bunco was freedom for me, if just for one night a month.

I will always remember that October Halloween bunco when there was a seismic shift in the group. Bunco would never be the same for me again. Looking back, I realize how much our conversations naturally changed over the years as our kids grew up, left the house, and went off on their own. In many ways there was less commonality.

We were no longer new to the community; we had branched out in different directions. I did not need the once-a-month escape like I had as a younger mom. The dispute started at the table in the dining room, but the commotion soon reached our card table in the family room. I recall the moment it got uncomfortable. I got up to walk into the dining room, ever the mediator. One woman stormed out of the house, another followed closely behind, followed by crying and total confusion. The ladies who were at the dining room table were shell shocked. One lady said, "I don't come to bunco to get in political arguments." There was no recovering; one by one, each woman slipped out of the house. Our friend had worked all day getting her house ready, cooking a fabulous dinner; arranging to have dad and the kids out of the house. Halloween bunco – what a disaster.

After that night bunco changed for me. It seemed that there were more substitutes; I guess I was not the only one who felt uncomfortable. For me, it was no longer the fun night out it used to be. The truth is I loved the ladies, but I did not want to know their politics, just as I did not care how much money they made. It was bunco — roll the dice, have a glass of wine, and laugh. Life is full of little boundaries. Eventually, I left the group with wonderful memories and some cherished friendships. I miss the days when money, religion, and politics were not considered polite topics for casual conversation.

Lunch drifted easily from topic to topic; these were friends that I could be honest with and expect honesty back. This is an important part of being a friend, enjoying meaningful conversation that moves effortlessly from serious to lighthearted. No one judging, no one pushing back, no one looking for a debate. How do we capture these moments to show our daughters? On the way home from that lunch,

I called my daughter and caught her up on the gossip, sharing how much we laughed and enjoyed each other. Right before I hung up, I added the real reason for my call: "It is so important to have female friends you respect and value and who feel the same way about you." All three of my children are used to my moments of contemplation. We learn by sharing.

Before we left the restaurant, we had the waiter take a picture, which I posted on my Facebook page and captioned 'Lunch and Laughter.' Remember to give your best to the people who give their best to you. There are five things that I have learned over time that have to be part of every relationship I have with a girlfriend. In many ways, they are boundaries that help me be a better friend and protect me from investing in relationships that will never work.

1. Different perspectives.

    Do not fear women with different perspectives. The world is divided enough, and women still face an uphill struggle, so do not purposely look for problems with other women. Spend your time searching for commonality. Learn to enjoy women who are different than you but have much to offer and are willing to share. I do not want to live in a bubble surrounded by women who tell me what I want to hear. I may never agree with your viewpoint, but I would rather be challenged in life than sidelined. I admit I struggle with this one the most.

2. Respect.

    Respect the women you welcome into your life. Respect their feelings, their accomplishments, and what they are doing professionally and personally. If you cannot celebrate a friend, then you are not a friend. Work hard on the issues that matter to you, but respect that others have their own paths. We do not have to be in lockstep with every person we invite to sit at our table, but I will not fear your judgment if I break bread with someone you disparage.

3. Mentoring.

My age has taught me that I do not know it all, nor will I ever be close. We should all crave learning, changing, improving. Gather around women who still want to learn, women who are investing in themselves and their happiness, women who are willing to talk candidly but are not easily offended. As we get older, we are faced with new issues, whether it is elderly parents, illness, death, or retirement. Surround yourself with women who have walked your path and are willing to share their experiences, the good, the bad, and the painful.

4. Honesty.

We suffocate in relationships where we cannot be honest; it is like walking on eggshells. The backlash will come; you just do not know when. True friends do not constantly move the goal posts, dishonest friends do. Do not wait to stab me when I turn around; look me in the eye when you do it. Being in a friendship with an emotionally dishonest person for too long makes you start to question reality. Often they are the ones who changed or got caught up in a new cause, but they have a way of twisting reality. Demand better for yourself. Without honesty there cannot be real friendship of any kind.

5. Loyalty.

    Loyalty has gone the way of chivalry. I was fortunate to see loyalty demonstrated by both my mother and father. My dad and I worked side by side for 24 years, and I watched how he made business deals, dealt with family, employees, and friends. Loyalty is earned, especially in friendship, but once it is earned, it is merited in return. There is a time and a season for most things, including friendships. Yes, sometimes we grow apart, and that is okay, but always value what you shared. Be loyal to what a friend meant to you when you trusted them to hear your most personal thoughts and struggles. Betrayal is petty. A person incapable of loyalty is not a person capable of true friendship.

    Boundaries are much like fences, and fences, so the saying goes, make good neighbors. I am reminded of my first and somewhat infamous (according to my family) TV appearance on our local Washington, DC, channel when I was six years old. I was invited to be on the Romper Room Show with Miss Connie. 'Do be a do bee, don't be a don't bee.' I was on the TV show for a week. We said the Pledge of Allegiance at the start of each show and prayed before our snack. We watched in excitement as Miss Connie held the Magic Mirror and told the kids watching from home that she could see them. During one show, Miss Connie asked, "What's new at your house today?" I announced that we were getting a fence for our backyard because my mom and dad were mad that our neighbors kept cutting through our yard and waving in our windows. My parents, watching from home with the entire neighborhood, were mortified; they still cringe today when retelling the story. But the new fence meant a dog, Shannon, a tricolored collie who was my first best friend. I guess fences, like boundaries, can be the start of something special.

Chapter 9
Lessons Learned from
Ex-Friends

"True friendship is not a one-
way street; it is not needy,
exhausting, obsessive or abusive.
A true friend values you as much
as you value them."

Real friendship takes a great deal of work, patience, honesty, and grace. I used to daydream that friendship was magical, effortless, perfect. Boy, was I wrong. Sometimes when a friendship ends there is no explanation; you simply grow apart, develop different interests – bad timing. Sometimes one of you changes and you no longer enjoy each other. Healthy friendships end with respect, a friendship with a mean girl ends with knives. I now know that there is tremendous value in learning from every relationship, especially those that end poorly. Do not allow yourself to be overwhelmed by self-pity and disappointment. Step back and ask yourself,

1. What attracted me to her in the first place?

2. Were there red flags that I chose to excuse?

3. How did she treat other women in her life?

4. Was I at my best or my worst with her?

5. How can I make better choices in the future?

Sometimes you must stop and ask yourself why a particular friend is so darn difficult to enjoy? Do not feel sorry for yourself; use your common sense. Do not wait around for the disaster to happen. Walk away or let the friendship fade out if it is not right for you. It is your responsibility to figure out what you need to do to make things better because, ultimately, you are making things better for yourself. View the end of a friendship as the beginning of a personal challenge. I am long past New Year's resolutions, but I do not miss a chance to reset when a poor choice trips me. Many ex-friends were probably never true friends. The word 'friend' is so overused that it is vanilla – mentor, colleague, bestie, friend, acquaintance, neighbor, companion, pal. It is hard to categorize every relationship that has come and gone. At times in my life, I have needed friends; at other times, I have wanted friends. Not best friends, just trusted women who offer support and get the same from me. But along the way we can experience some very odd interactions in an effort to do what we have been taught to do since we were little girls – make friends.

Occasionally you hit it off with a woman who is the perfect fit, but the timing misses the mark. I refer to these as startup friendships; we have all experienced them. They are so promising, but they never quite get off the ground. I will never forget meeting the coolest woman who checked off every box. She was interesting, funny, and very genuine. I am bragging, we had a lot in common, except one big thing, age. I was 16 years older than she was, and while I consider myself young at heart, lol, we were in completely different seasons of our lives. I was a newbie empty nester with a great deal of recently found time, and control over my day. I had been where she was, a long time ago. Her schedule was frenzied, juggling children, a promising career and after school activities. I could see that being friends with me in any meaningful way would take time she did not have.

My years of trying to balance it all had taught me to appreciate people based on the value they bring to my life, not the amount of time they spend with me. After letting women like this 'move on' in the past, I decided that there should be a place for them in my life. They are my friendly acquaintances, women I rarely see but am always grateful when I do. She quite naturally fell into that space. We reach out when there is drama over our shared interests (fun drama). She is loyal and trustworthy, and it is so entertaining to have a good gossip session with her. Like me, she relishes strategizing and maneuvering. She finds the 'what ifs' delightful, like a fine wine. I admire her brain, gumption, and oomph. We have settled into an occasional text friendship; that is all the time she has, and I am good with that. Once in a while we make plans to meet, but that never seems to work out for one reason or another – no blame, just reality. I value her friendship for what it is. I wish I had learned earlier how to maintain friendships like this. I have not put her on the shelf; I have saved her a seat at my table with no expectations, just appreciation for the value she adds to my life every time our paths cross. This woman will have more time when her children are grown, and I will look forward to it.

Sometimes you hit it off with a woman who is a perfect fit, but nothing is what it seems. One of my oddest start-up friendships happened when I was in my early 40s. I was introduced to a group of dynamic women undertaking a large charitable project. I was new in town and hoping to get involved in the community and make new friends. Moving to Texas to join my parents' business was my family's final move after a decade in the military – a chance to settle in, grow roots, and belong. This philanthropic effort was the perfect opportunity to meet ladies my age, while giving back to a cause in which I believed. The committee meetings were held at a local coffee shop. Eight women gathered around three café tables, casually shoved together – our kingdom. After an hour plus of lattes, updates, and assignments, we raced out like we had raced in, everyone off in different directions. After our second meeting, a couple of women lingered, and the chatter shifted from business to pleasure. I gravitated toward a woman who I can only describe as jolly. She had a huge smile that seemed painted on her face, and a loud but sincere laugh. Welcoming, yes, she was over the top welcoming, and I loved that. Everyone in the group knew her and liked her. During our third coffee shop huddle, she and I were assigned a joint task. For the next few months we were a team. I really enjoyed her, and together we were doing a bang-up job for the philanthropy, that was what mattered most.

When we were not meeting with the committee, she invited me to grab lunch at least once a week, plus phone calls and daily messages.

Conversation became familiar: kids, school, shopping, advice. There was no tiptoeing from partnership to friendship; we went right to fireworks. I admit it was a bit overwhelming; I can only handle so much closeness, but I felt certain that when the project wrapped up, we would fall into a more normal friendship, certainly one that was less arduous. Well, I got my wish. When the project ended, the woman who had worked so hard to become my friend for three months disappeared. I was ghosted. According to the Oxford Dictionary, ghosting is "the practice of ending a personal relationship with someone by suddenly withdrawing from all communication."

I sent her an email after a week of zero contact, and as I recall, I left a message, "Just wanted to check in, hope you have recovered!" Nothing. This was pre-Facebook so there was no page stalking to see if she was still alive. I did not know what to think; she was all hugs one day and gone the next. Honestly, I was a bit relieved the first few days when I did not hear from her; I needed a rest since for me it had been too much attention. I was looking forward to being friends without the pressure of a project. Little did I know we were only friends because of the project. I had no interest in being creepy, but all I could imagine was that she had gotten sick. I ran into one of the other committee members at my daughter's school. Maybe she knew something? Yes, all was well; they were actually getting together the following week to start planning a gala in the fall. I cannot imagine the look on my face. Ironically, she asked if I would like to join the gala committee – surreal moment. Now that would be awkward. Yes, I had begun to figure out that I had been dumped.

At least two months went by before I saw my old friend again. I was picking up lunch at a restaurant across the street from my office

– chicken breast, broccoli, and a baked sweet potato, no butter. One of my healthy eating phases. I had called ahead and raced in to grab my to-go order at the bar. Two decades before COVID, there was no curbside. I was stopped dead in my tracks when I heard the laugh. Panic. Quick, grab my order, and sneak out through the side door. Instead, I froze. Here goes nothing, I turned and anxiously eased myself into the dining room. She was engrossed in conversation with, you guessed it, the woman I ran into at my daughter's school. I wanted to throw up. Right before my eyes, I completely understood her tactics.

I had fallen for a pro. How did she react when I walked up to the table? Her painted smile grew larger than life as she jumped up and wrapped me in a bear hug. My nonsensical words tumbled over my tongue; she never skipped a beat. There was no happy ending; she had moved on to a new project and a new friend. I was embarrassed and felt cast off. Three months later, I attended the gala; the 'friends' shared the stage, both dressed beautifully (hair, makeup, smiles). Together, they floated around the lavish event as if conducting an orchestra. That was the last night of their friendship. I admit that I felt strangely vindicated when I ran into my 'replacement' at the grocery store weeks after the gala. She was still reeling but had come to terms with the fact that she had been dumped. When the project is over, so are you.

Fast forward 14 years. I had just been elected mayor. Out of the blue, I received an email:

Hey old friend, it's been way too long. Congratulations! We are so happy for you. We need to celebrate soon. You probably remember my son XXXX, he graduates next year, can you believe it? Where has the time gone? XXXX is putting together college applications and I immediately thought of you. He is going to reach out to you. I have attached his resume.

Love you! XXXXX

Hahaha, what are old friends for? Fourteen years, not a word; now I am mayor and look who is back. Ironically – well, not really – she did not even vote in the election. Did I write the letter for her son? Yes, my Catholic guilt. I guess that was the right thing to do, but I certainly did not do it for her. I did it for myself. I needed a win. She emailed me one last time thanking me for the college recommendation and asking me to send her some dates so she could buy me a thank-you lunch. I hit delete. That was the end of it, no surprise.

Sometimes you hit it off with a woman who is a perfect fit, but you slowly start to realize she 'needs' you and she is not going anywhere as long as you are available. Who has not escaped a needy friend? She needs you all the time –your help, your support, a shoulder to cry on, an ear to listen. Sounds normal? Well, it is until you need her. For the friendship to work, you are expected to be on call, respond to texts immediately, and always be 100% engaged in whatever her issue is. Everything goes along smoothly until suddenly you need 100% from her. That is when things get tricky. Her life always seems to be more demanding than yours. Her kid is suddenly sick . . . again, her husband needs his dry cleaning picked up; well maybe not that obvious a brush off, but there is always an issue. She would be there for you if only . . . You have to accept that the needy friend makes the rules. The friendship works if you do not need as much from her as she needs from you. It will end, mark my words; no friendship can survive long-term with such an imbalance. The key is to spot it sooner so you do not invest too much time and energy in this dead-end relationship. Do not sugarcoat or make excuses; pulling back will tell you all you need to know. If they want the friendship, they will want to earn it back, but do not hold your breath. They will just find someone else. We all know these women, just watch their social media. They never have the same friend for very long. Too needy often means too selfish.

Anytime you find yourself socializing regularly in a group large or small, be aware of how everyone is treated. I was part of an informal lunch group many years ago (which seems to be a theme with me). It was a chance to stay up-to-date on all the latest news and gossip. Just fun. Over time, I started to sense that one woman was being pushed out. Whenever we scheduled lunch, it appeared that everyone's schedule mattered except hers. At a few of our gatherings, there seemed to be an odd vibe. I realized that the slights were on purpose and aimed at one women. I regret not speaking up before it was too late. The woman who was targeted stopped coming to lunch. The group only lasted a few more months, the organizers had formed their own little clique and lost interest in our lunch group. It turns out that one of them did not like the woman who had been pushed out. I had to own all the little slights that I had pretended not to notice. Lesson learned: it is not okay to sit by and say nothing; you must speak up.

I was sliding into a tiny red vinyl booth in a small family-owned Italian restaurant near my office. It was a few weeks before Christmas, and the restaurant had decked the halls. Silver garland bursting with shiny red and green ornaments crisscrossed the ceiling. Christmas trees draped with twinkling lights were stuffed into each corner of the restaurant. Every table celebrated with its own pink plastic poinsettia. Today I was having lunch with a dear friend, someone who has known me for 25 years. Like many of my friends, she and her husband are semi-retired and spend most of their time traveling. When we see each other, we pick up right where we left off, regardless of how much time has passed. Maybe it was the overflowing holiday spirit in the restaurant or simply the essence of the season, but our conversation drifted back to when we met all those years ago. We talked about raising our children, now young adults. We laughed and reminisced, getting stuck on old memories and spending ten minutes trying to recall faded details. The conversation settled on one particular ex-friend.

My dear friend looked me directly in the eye and said, "I used to feel a little envious when you would refer to her as one of your best friends. I was always there for you, but you did not refer to me the same way. I never understood why because everyone could see that she really didn't care about you as much as you cared about her." She went on to remind me about one event she had never forgotten. It was the annual fundraiser for a philanthropic organization that was very important to me. This particular year was special. I was chairman of their board and one of the luncheon sponsors. I invited nine ladies, including my daughter, to be my guests. All the ladies met at my office the morning of the event; everyone was dressed up and excited for the day ahead. I even rented a limousine to drive us to downtown Fort Worth. As we were gathering in my office lobby, I got a last-second call: my 'friend' would not be able to make it. It was not the first time and it would not be the last. I just chose not to be realistic about our relationship.

Sitting in that booth, listening to my friend, I knew she was right. Listen to your family, trusted friends, and colleagues when they raise red flags. My dad and I worked together for 24 years. I have a dear friend who has since retired and moved away but my dad always enjoyed when she came by our office. He would pop his head in my office and jokingly say, "Can someone please give this woman a job. She works harder than Laura." My dad did not feel the same way about others who stopped in. Listen to the people who mean the most to you. Most importantly, trust your gut. True friendship is not a one-way street. A true friend values you as much as you value them.

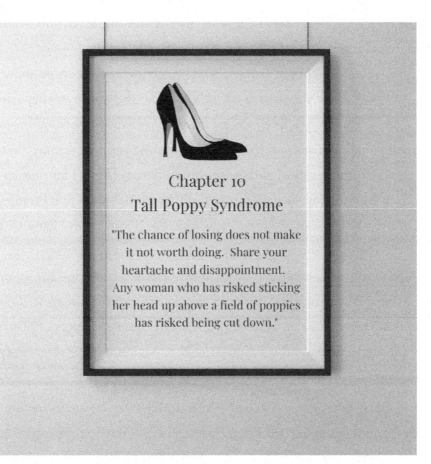

Chapter 10
Tall Poppy Syndrome

"The chance of losing does not make
it not worth doing. Share your
heartache and disappointment.
Any woman who has risked sticking
her head up above a field of poppies
has risked being cut down."

I am up early, crossing Magazine Street, headed to Audubon Park, hoping to get in a good walk before the Louisiana humidity starts to rise, and the scorching sun finds a way to slip through the spider web of massive oak limbs dripping with moss. I pass the stables, then the zoo, finally blending in with the other early morning walkers, most with dogs or baby carriages. My AirPods are streaming a true crime podcast (I am obsessed). I consider my podcast app a treasure chest of whodunnits and whys. 'Saturday Night Live' did a hysterical skit a few years back about women who are obsessed with crime shows and cannot wait for their husbands to leave the house so they can immerse themselves in the latest murder mystery, absorbing every grisly detail. Believe me, the obsession is real. I stream a show, then download the podcast, and down the rabbit hole I go. This particular morning, I was listening to *L.A. Not So Confidential*, 'The Premier Forensic Psychology Podcast,' episode 124, Toxic Sports Parents. I am a Texan, home to Friday Night Lights and The Positively True Adventures of the Alleged Texas Cheerleader Murdering Mom, or in simpler English, the Wanda Holloway murder for hire case. This episode was a series of cases that revolved around kid sports. Sports-motivated assaults and attempted murders – parents living vicariously through their children's sports performance.

The host was providing background for the Texas cheerleader case and referencing 'tall poppy syndrome.' Where had I heard that before? He referred to it as a Southern phrase, ah yes, my college days. I remember two girls in Main Hall, senior year at R-MWC, privately debating, one girl accusing the other of having 'tall poppy syndrome.' Back then, the only thing I knew about poppies was the massive field of indistinguishable red flowers in the movie *The Wizard of Oz*. The Wicked Witch of the West put a spell on Dorothy, the Tin Man, Scarecrow, Cowardly Lion, and Toto in a huge field of poppies, with Glinda, the good witch of the South, saving them.

The Tall Poppy Syndrome was first popularized in Australia by Susan Mitchell's 1984 book, Tall Poppies. It became a cultural phenomenon critical of groupthink and of the risk of being cut down for standing out. In nature, poppies grow to a standard, almost identical, height. If an errant poppy grows taller than the rest of the field, it will be strangled by the shorter poppies. Tall Poppy Syndrome occurs when a person's success is a reason for them to be attacked, resented, or criticized for standing out in the crowd, or worse, above it. If you are ridiculed for overachieving and discouraged from being unique, you will learn to accept mediocrity from yourself and others. Women do not want to be a target of criticism, gossip, or strangulation!

I am a believer in Tall Poppy Syndrome; I have seen it firsthand. So how do women, especially in the workplace, combat this? The first step is that we must give our female coworkers the same benefit of the doubt that we give our male coworkers. Women must be honest; we view other women's accomplishments more critically than those of our male colleagues. We are harsh in our judgment and stingy with our praise. We are trained from the time we are little that girls are our competition and boys are the prize. We spend so much time trying to fit in and not be a tall poppy that we do not learn how to appreciate other women's accomplishments, especially when they achieve much bigger things than we do. The success of women is consistently downplayed, and so the cycle continues. As women, we do young females a huge disservice by not mentoring them to anticipate the myriad of emotions and experiences they will encounter. They are going to have disappointments in life, and many of those disappointments are going to be in the workplace. Getting let down by a girlfriend hurts, but not being supported by your female co-workers is a professional gut punch. Women, in effect, give power over to men when we step back from the limelight because we want to fit in, not make waves, not stand out. Men do not operate that way; they pat each other on the back, buy each other a beer, and move on.

For those women who battle to the top, there is often an uncontrollable impulse to batten down the hatches and protect their position at all costs. We have watched women on our own journey reach the top. We have heard the gossip, seen the backstabbing, and tasted the sour grapes. So why would we have any different expectations when we get to the top? I have spoken about not pulling the ladder up when you get to the top, but if we want successful women to reach down and pull us up, we have to be trustworthy, honest, and dedicated. If you are a woman who cannot be trusted, mentors will steer clear of you. You must be intentional. Remember, you are always being judged by someone at some level. Be a woman that other women want to help. I am not suggesting you change who you are at the core or fake it, but you may have to ease up. Do not take things personally, be a team player, do not wear your emotions all over your face, and treat your colleagues fairly. I have learned the hard way that being inflexible and intense can be off-putting. It has taken years, but I finally learned that I needed to lighten up – on myself and on others. Now, I applaud the achievements of other women and use their success to fuel me to aim higher. You are not a mean girl for being envious, you are a mean girl when envy turns to spite.

Sometimes it takes something monumental to get your attention. I had always had a tough time managing my expectations of everyone, including myself. It took the end of my 17-year marriage to finally realize how much my own expectations were exhausting me. I became a single mom with three children, a dog, and a business; divorce had given me time for much needed self-reflection. If I could stop being so hard on myself and trying to control everything around me, maybe all my relationships would be easier. In a small business, there is nowhere to hide. Everyone had to deal with me, so it was a priority to make sure the work environment was not stressful because of me. Women often get caught up in thinking that if everything looks perfect they must have it under control. How many times have we stressed over things that do not matter? How many times have we vacuumed the house rather than spent time with family and friends? Life is meant to be wrinkled, not perfectly pressed. Here are five lessons that helped me slow down and give myself grace:

1. Be intentional.

    No matter what ladder you are climbing, you need a mentor/sponsor. It is not negotiable. You need at least one person who knows you well enough to be able to make the case that you are the real deal. If you do not have a mentor or sponsor willing to spend their personal or professional capital on you, it may not matter that you are the most qualified. The bar for women is higher. We have to be overqualified and have a proven track record. Even then, we are judged more harshly. That is why sponsors and mentors are currency. Your mentors are money in the bank, people who will use their influence and good name to connect you and promote you. Build key relationships, be intentional, and invest in people who are willing to invest in you. There is nothing fake about it. Successful leaders leverage all the resources they can, and people are a key resource.

    You must be intentional about building professional relationships and developing trusted colleagues and mentors. Do your research, join professional organizations and associations, expand your search beyond your immediate field; look for the best of the best, the folks that are admired and respected. Meet women through shared causes and interests. The more they get to know you in a relaxed setting, the greater the probability that they will speak positively about you when you are not in the room. Frequency of touch is what helps you build a long-standing, invested relationship. If there is someone you want to build a relationship with, find meaningful ways to intersect with them. Never be afraid to pick up the phone and extend an invitation.

Can you recover a connection with a mentor or sponsor if you have failed them? Yes, if you mean it and own it. Be authentic, humble, take responsibility and do not say 'but.' Ask for an opportunity to repair the relationship and earn back trust. It is too easy to walk away, especially for women, who generally dislike emotional confrontations. It is hard to admit your shortcomings but if the relationship brings you value, suck it up and fight for it. Do not expect to be welcomed back with open arms, but make it clear you will prove yourself. So many failed friendships and business relationships could be fixed with a little humility. We must lose with class and win with grace. Be a woman who supports the tall poppies.

2. Be a collaborator.

   As a mentor, co-worker, colleague, or friend, collaboration is vital because it builds more powerful results and stronger associations. A leader must create that synergy, an environment for partnership, where everyone has a seat at the table to participate in a meaningful way. Regardless of how small the role is, everyone needs to feel that they are contributing. Leaders share the stage. The win is everyone's; the loss is theirs. The more you are willing to collaborate, the more you will create an atmosphere where trust, dedication and loyalty flourish. Be generous with praise, generous with listening, and generous with gratitude for a job well done. Collaboration produces real authenticity. View each member of every team as a social media post going out and spreading the word about you and your style. Your standing will rise with theirs.

3. Be professional.

Be professional during each interaction, or you risk only being remembered for the times you were not. Mistakes can cost you dozens of customers and relationships without you even knowing it. I had the oddest experience in an upscale clothing store just around the corner from my house in New Orleans. It was a hot, humid June Saturday; even with SPF 50, it felt like every inch of exposed skin was frying. I left the house dressed in cropped jeans, a crisp white T-shirt (well, it was crisp when I left the house), comfortable shoes, and a baseball cap. I was ready to spend the entire day shopping and eating my way along my favorite street in New Orleans. Magazine Street stretches for six miles from Canal Street to Audubon Park, weaving through the Central Business District, the historic Garden District, and Uptown. An eclectic mix of homes, shops, restaurants and art galleries cohabiting harmoniously side by side as if holding each other up. I pass PJ's coffee shop, where I wrote most of my first book, and ESOM gallery, where I purchased my first original painting by Tony Mose, Hazelnut, owned by actor Bryan Batt who played Salvatore Romano, from Mad Men fame. The first time I ever went into his store, he was there working behind the counter, and he told me that he loved my shoes (a cute pair of navy and gray Vince slip-ons). I was so excited; he made a great customer for life. It is the little things.

Jumping on the St. Charles Street trolley at the 6300 block, in front of Tulane and Loyola University, I rode all the way down to the 2000 block, where I hopped off and meandered south along Josephine, admiring the stately homes as I make my way to Magazine. First stop; Miette: a tiny shop packed with vibrant Mardi Gras float flowers from floor to ceiling. I crisscrossed Magazine for hours exploring all my favorite shops, taking in the architecture, a Po-boy at Guy's, and a pastry from La Boulangerie. By the time I was nearing home, it was late afternoon. One last stop was a tony clothing store where the air-conditioning felt luxurious. I looked a bit worse for wear – hot, sweaty, embarrassingly so – but determined to check out their dresses. A knee length navy dress caught my eye. As I lifted the dress off the hanger, I caught the attention of the saleswoman. She had not greeted me when I entered the department; I assume she was a bit concerned to see a sweaty woman handling their clothing. She was petit; her hair was chin-length and flipped under casually but purposefully, kept nicely in place by a plaid head band. She looked to be about my age but had let her hair go gray. A button-down blouse, pearls pressed khaki slacks, and Kate Spade flats finished off the very classic look. I know the stink eye when I see it, and she was giving it to me. She asked half-heartedly if I wanted to start a dressing room. I had no interest in trying on clothes in my state. I was heading home to Texas the next day, so if I saw something I had to have, I would grab it and try it on later, after a shower. "No, I just want to look." She seemed relieved. I spotted a rolling rack of dresses, still in plastic, as though they had just arrived. A bright red dress with short sleeves, caught my eye. As I took the dress off the rack, she scurried over and took it from me and stated as a matter of fact, "The dresses on this rack are for younger women. Most are short sleeved or sleeveless. I have another rack in the back with long sleeves and ¾ sleeves, better suited for an older woman's arms."

Seriously? I will buy whatever the heck I want to buy; I do not need your opinion about my arms. As for my age, I have a great color job, Botox, and my mom's incredible genetics, not to mention hours in the gym. So, I doubt you can come close to guessing my age. My brain was imploding; the words were rolling into my mouth where, they were swallowed. Praying to the karma gods, I gave her a fake smile; her day would come, but it would not be today. I left unceremoniously, walked the few blocks home, sat on the front porch, and contemplated paybacks with a bag of Zapp's Voodoo potato chips.

I could have bought that pricy red dress and made her day, if she had just been professional, and taken some time to make small talk. Instead, she made a series of unfortunate assumptions. Costly assumptions for her since she was paid on commission. Four weeks later, I went back to that store. This time it was my only stop. I wanted to look at those red dresses again. I was hoping she would be there and that she was not the only clerk in the department. I got my wish. I beelined it to the rack of red, white, and blue dresses (it was now July), hanging on a permanent rack. A young woman scurried over to welcome me and proceeded to make friendly small talk. I bought two dresses that day; my favorite, the red one, is the dress I wore in my official mayor portrait (yes, the infamous dry cleaner red dress). The woman who had been so opinionated wandered over as I was paying and asked, "Didn't I help you a few weeks ago?" "Help me? No," I replied. Both dresses had ¾ length sleeves; yes, I know what looks good on 'women my age.'

4. Be a listener.

I love it when an unplanned conversation changes you and how you judge another person. My advice, make opportunities for yourself to sit down and have meaningful conversations with women in your larger circle that you admire. We spend too much time imagining and not enough time asking; you never know what path someone else has walked. Invite them for a cup of coffee. What is the worst thing that can happen? They say no. I had the chance to sit down with a woman who I have admired from afar for years. We knew of each other, and had mutual friends, but had never interacted beyond simple niceties, and likes on Facebook. Honestly, I was intimidated by her. She exudes confidence, is always perfectly put together, is successful, and is a huge community supporter. If I had not gotten the nerve to invite her for coffee, I would have missed out on hearing about her amazing journey. She shared with me her motivating force. A woman unafraid of standing out, being the tall poppy. Driven to give herself every opportunity that she was not afforded as a child. She grew up neglected and unloved. The adults in her life were cruel and selfish. She did not understand how deep the abuse was until she was old enough to have friends, have sleepovers, and share secrets. Gradually and uncomfortably, she realized that her life was not normal and that there were things happening in her home that did not happen in friends' homes. Imagine thinking that abuse was a normal occurrence in every family; imagine believing that because it was all you have ever known.

She shared how nervous she was about having coffee with me, how much she looked up to me. Seriously? When I confessed how starstruck I had always been about her, she laughed out loud. Making the time made all the difference, for both of us. I judged her by what I saw on the outside – the mystique of perfection. In truth, it was a pronouncement that her future would not mirror her past. Do not be quick to make assumptions about successful women; invest the time to learn more about them. We all know women who seem perfectly put together. They are pretty, smart, ambitious, and successful. Do not envy them; learn from them. Make small talk, listen, and find commonality. Bonding in simple but meaningful ways builds trust, which can develop into intentional relationships.

5. Be fearless

Not everyone can win all the time, and as hard as you try, there will be plenty of losses along your journey. How do you keep moving forward and continuing to work on the things that are important to you when you hit roadblocks, experience a setback or things just do not go your way? Too often women make decisions not to do something because they are afraid of losing or afraid of letting other people down. Yes, losing can be devastating. Yet it is absolutely part of being a healthy human being. If you want it, the chance to succeed makes it worth trying. If you lose, own your heartache and disappointment with honesty and hopefulness. Any woman who has risked sticking her head up above a field of poppies, has risked being cut down. Ultimately, we will always have some amount of fear or trepidation about attempting hard things. Your goal should not be avoiding fear or constantly trying to overcome it. View fear as a challenge, jump in there and give it all you have; it is what women do best.

How do we raise daughters who are fearless? We must spend intentional time talking one-on-one and in person. We impart so much wisdom just from the tone of our voice, making eye contact, or giving a nod. Sharing our successes and disappointments in an age-appropriate way is vital. Do not think that your daughter cannot understand present issues in a way that makes sense for her age. Be deliberate. Teaching our girls how to talk through issues must start at a very young age. Learning to handle small problems builds upon itself and helps develop resiliency so that bigger challenges are not insurmountable. Yes, there will certainly be frustration, sadness, disappointment, betrayal, and anger. Fearless women do not hide or pretend; they tap into their friends and mentors and navigate a way forward.

There is a woman I know who always sits at a table for one. She chooses to sit alone so that she has the perfect vantage point to criticize everything happening around her. She seems to particularly dislike other women and watches for any chance to put them down. She boasts that she would have done better but never tries. As her daughter's greatest role model, what example does she set by constantly watching for missteps by others? By demonstrating that tall poppies need to be destroyed, she is teaching her daughter to steer clear of being fearless. There is too much risk in aiming up if someone is always watching, ready to cut you back down to size (someone like her mother). I would rather raise a daughter to be a woman who is confident in making her own decisions and not paralyzed by fear of criticism, a daughter who has seen me fight to the finish, win or lose. Our daughters are walking into a completely different world than we did. It should not be a miracle that they have the tools to navigate through the ups and downs of life. Raise young women unafraid to grow above the field.

Chapter 11
The Tightrope

"Be honest about your strengths and weaknesses. Accept that the road to success looks different for everyone, especially women."

My circle of close female friends is small, but they are the pillars that support a larger group of casual friends and acquaintances. Surround yourself with women who let you breathe, and do not let mean girls creep into your inner circle. Mean girls demand proximity; they work slowly and methodically and have a way of making you feel bad for saying no. How foolish to refuse the help and support of someone so seemingly bighearted. You learn to go along to get along because disagreeing with them becomes a beatdown. After all, you must be ungrateful; they are just trying to support you. Once they ease their way into your inner circle of friends and associates, they gradually take over. They do this by claiming to be speaking for you, or insinuating they were told to call on your behalf; they present themselves using the terms like 'best friend' or 'closest associate.' Slowly, systematically, your friends and colleagues become theirs. They are textbook manipulators who are always offering up valuable support, information or hot gossip to lure you in, but they want access in return. That is the currency in which they trade.

What you eventually realize is that the price they demand is your constant attention and complete allegiance. These women want to be friends with you because of your position and connections. They put tremendous energy into you, disguised as friendship, but do not mistake it for a caring relationship. Believe me, they make you feel good about the job you are doing and the decisions you are making, but only if they have a role. Eventually, their communications with you will change from conversational to demanding and critical. They believe that your success is overwhelmingly due to their support. These women seem to thrive on being seen as powerful influencers; they brainwash you into believing you owe them, and if you dare change the terms, there will be payback.

Whether you hold a corporate position, own a business, or serve in an elected position, the buck stops with you. If you want to be successful, you cannot hand over accountability. You have a job to do; yes, many people have helped and supported you over the years, but it is your name on the letterhead. Do not make the mistake of going into a new job believing you owe allegiance first to a friend or colleague because they supported you. The position and the obligations that go with it are the priority. Many women worry too much about making a misstep, they want to make everyone happy and to be popular, so they are quick to allow others to step in and share the decision-making responsibility. Oh, the price you will pay.

The workplace is not the ideal place for girlfriends; it is actually very dicey. You should keep your work life separate from your personal life. A woman reached out to me after a speaking engagement, I will call her Sally. She offered to share the story of a painful breakup with her best friend, whom I will call Ellen—a breakup that cost her the company she had built and set her back years in her industry. Sally met Ellen through an introduction at a regional business mixer. Both women were go-getters; each had started their own small companies in the same industry. Sally admits that she really liked Ellen from day one. They were understandably cautious about getting to know each other because they competed for many of the same clients. For over a year, their relationship patiently grew, and they started socializing outside of industry luncheons and networking events. Professional conversation eased into personal sharing. Over time, they became inseparable. Sally ran into some financial struggles that were affecting her family and business. Ellen was always there to offer a hand. She insisted on picking up lunch tabs, attending client meetings, and finishing up Sally's paperwork. If Sally said no, Ellen would pout; it was not worth the hassle, so she reluctantly let Ellen take over more and more. One night, after several cocktails (Sally's words), they threw caution to the wind and decided to become 'casual' business partners.

No contract was necessary; they were best friends. Sally was desperate for a steady income, just until she could get back on her feet. Ellen offered to put Sally on her payroll. Sally let the lease on her office go and moved her company in with Ellen's. She insisted on contributing to the rent; Ellen would not hear of it. Yes, we know where this ends. The lines between business and friendship continued to blur. Sally felt blessed that Ellen had come into her life. With Ellen's encouragement, Sally concentrated on her family and spent less time at the office or doing her job. Ellen had all the time and space she needed to slowly and methodically replace Sally with her friends, clients, and colleagues.

One morning, Sally arrived at their shared office space to find that her key did not work. Her call to Ellen received a text response: "My lawyer will be in touch to set up a meeting." Sally texted and called her best friend for hours, but there was no response. At the meeting with Ellen and her attorney, Sally was terminated, offered a severance package, and presented with an NDA (non-discloser agreement). When Sally pleaded with Ellen and begged her to give her client files back, the attorney spoke for Ellen. There was no contract, and no written agreement; it was over. Take it or leave it.

A decade has passed since the meeting in that attorney's office, but I could feel the gut punch as Sally shared her devastation. She barely recovered; her marriage did not. Whispers around the industry, started by you know who, painted Sally as problem-ridden. Her friends, clients, and colleagues were now Ellen's. Sally was the target of a mean girl, a cruel and devious woman who planned every step. Ellen is still running her business; she has had several other clashes over the years. She spends a lot of time being sued. Sally left the industry and started over, determined but untrusting. Professional embarrassment can be devastating to your sense of self. Sally was vulnerable; her eye was off the ball, which made her the perfect target for the worst kind of mean girl. Our conversation was painful; she even offered me references to check out her story. She was well aware that it sounded farfetched – how could a friend be so willfully malicious? Sally is still embarrassed and disheartened after all these years.

No one thinks this can happen to them. Women in particular let their emotions play too big a role in their decision-making process. I say this with no judgment; it is an opportunity to learn and to help others dodge the same disaster. The 'morning after' the ladies decided to partner up, Sally needed one of her mentors. It is no different than getting a second opinion when faced with a medical decision. Anytime you contemplate taking a risk, especially one that seems too good to be true, seek out a mentor who will challenge you. Your mentors ensure that your decision-making is based on facts, not fantasy. Their guidance can steer you clear of a mean girl. If you find yourself shortcutting your tried-and-true processes, hit the brakes.

1. If you are not at your best, hit pause.

2. Make your decisions based on facts not fantasy.

3. Seek out trusted mentors and colleagues who will challenge your enthusiasm.

4. If it is business, see a lawyer.

5. Take your time (days, weeks or months) with every big decision.

Invest, invest, invest. Work hard to cultivate your relationships with your mentors and trusted colleagues; you want them on speed dial. Respect professional boundaries: they are not girlfriends to have a drink with after work and gossip about office politics. Women need a network of like-minded females who want to help them without strings attached. Be a woman who other women want to advise and support. Keep emotionally based relationships out of the office. Whenever there is a power shift, there is a heightened risk of jealousy, hurt feelings, sabotage, or payback. We are little girls at heart, and too much emotional sharing in the wrong setting always gets us in trouble.

I have only had one close female friendship in my life that I now understand was toxic. Where has that word been all my life? I am actually grateful that there is a word that helps me understand why she needed to "pay me back." (Yes, her words.) Although that was just the tip of the iceberg, it is uncomfortable to admit that someone could say those words about me and mean them. Maybe I should find comfort in knowing that I am not her only victim. I have moved on, but I still struggle with the people who think they are doing me a 'favor' stalking her every dig against me. They send screen shots or midnight text messages. "You are not going to believe this . . ." I have learned to hit delete and then reply with the 'crazy' emoji. But we all know women who seem to delight in telling us that another woman said or did something unkind behind our backs or posted something hurtful. Do they think they are doing you a favor? We should all be allowed to move on; do not be the person who keeps the drama stirred up. No matter how confident or successful a woman is, it hurts. Believe me.

During my first decade in the hospitality industry, I wore tailored Brooks Brothers suits, crisp white button-downs, low pumps (no heels), and finished the look off with a silk bow that gave a nod to a men's tie. I wanted to be like the guys on the fast track. They wore navy blue suits, polished loafers, and silk ties, they all had a quick smile and a firm handshake. As I viewed it, they got by with less talent but more charm – an exclusive club where the men watched out for each other. Of course, it was hospitality; I should have been shrewder. But I learned much watching how the male managers supported each other; there was no drama. If there was workplace competitiveness, they hid it. The men seemed to be all in for each other; the women, not so much. In my early career in hospitality, I miscalculated because I did not understand that I could not power through every situation with just the force of my will and motivation to out-work everyone else. I chose to be the bull in the china shop and justified it with the results. As a wiser woman, I can see that my motivation, ambition, and tough personality made me 'difficult' in the eyes of male bosses. I needed them on my side in order to achieve my goals. I needed to learn finesse.

The irony was not lost on anyone that whenever a hotel was opening up, closing down, or going through significant problems, the company sent me. I remember when Stouffer bought the old Americana Hotel on the Genesee River in Rochester, New York. The hotel had been unionized; the plan after a lengthy and expensive remodel was to reopen as a nonunion hotel. Yes, they sent me. I savored the challenge, the stress, and the intensity. We were successful and I had found my niche. I climbed the ladder by making my own track and taking the tough assignments – the jobs the fast-track guys did not want. Never be afraid to acknowledge your strengths and use them to pivot. Accept that the road to success looks different for everyone, especially women.

I almost sabotaged my career trying to be one of the guys. Be careful what you wish for. Women have given so much of their power away by trying to be more like men. We made a huge mistake by allowing the 'sexual revolution' to redefine womanhood. We were told that we had to act like men, dress like men, and make decisions like men. Over the last few decades, the women's movement has empowered women to believe that they can do things their way. An extension of this newly found 'you do you' is that some women have unwisely brought sexuality into the workplace by the way they dress. Sure, express yourself and be empowered to 'do you', but do not make the mistake of believing that there is no price to be paid. You can be stylish without miniskirts or unbuttoning your shirt so that your bra becomes part of the look. What you post on Saturday night is what people see on Monday morning. When you open your closet, know that you can be gorgeous, classy, and in charge without 'your body' being the most important ingredient. It all plays into the dynamic of little girls on the playground. Judging each other's looks, weight, and clothes. Attractive to men, antagonizing to other women. Lessons learned long ago as a little girl. Am I popular or not? Am I pretty or not? Am I good enough or not? I think back to those parties – the ones I did not get invited to.

Women walk a tightrope, wanting to appear professional and classy but also eager to express themselves. In the back of our minds, we understand that women quite naturally judge each other – always. I had a female Facebook friend (that was the extent of our relation-ship) private message me after an event: "I searched the internet and finally found the dress you wore last night?!" Followed by "WOW, I hope you bought it on sale!" What man has EVER received an email or message like that? It is no wonder women second guess everything we say, do, and wear. Women can be very unkind to other women, but mean girls can be brutal. We have all been left out, not chosen, and not invited. We have been the subject of giggling and pointing. Mean girls are not solely guilty of the occasional snub or slight; face it, all women have had their mean moments. Mean girls are different; there is intentional planning that seems to define them. They lack empathy, and worse, they delight in causing discomfort and anguish to other women. I remember speaking at an event when my eyes locked in on one of the mean girls; she was there with her orders: record everything I said, with fingers crossed that I would say something that could be used against me. As soon as I was done speaking, she zipped out through the crowd. Not very stealthily, certainly not very clever, but a dutiful follower.

We set examples for our daughters every single day by what we post, how we talk on the phone, the kind of friends we surround ourselves with, and how we treat those friends. We must raise our daughters to be empathetic. If a woman can be purposely cruel to other women, what kind of women will her daughters grow up to be? What kind of woman will her sons grow up to love? You teach your daughter how to be the best woman she can be: a good friend, confident, independent, understanding, and resilient. We hold our daughters' and sons' futures in our hands on so many levels.

In the category of I have seen it all. I was headed to town hall to meet with a mother and daughter. The mom had made the appointment on behalf of her daughter. I was expecting a request for a college recommendation. When I took the elevator to the 4th floor and walked through the double doors embossed with 'Office of the Mayor.' I was not sure what to expect. It was immediately apparent that mom and daughter had grown to five — two moms and three teenage girls. Holy cow. Fortunately, hello came out of my mouth instead. Memories flooded back to the table of four tennis moms years earlier. The cute little pizza and wine bar. The three lieutenants receiving their orders. "We are done with her; I never liked her anyway. You need to stop calling and texting her." The nod as they passed our table. I remembered wondering what people would think of those four women if they were privy to their treatment of 'her.' Childhood memories flooded back. Four mean girls – all grown up. For a split second in that little restaurant, I wanted to say something, admit my eavesdropping, and defend the poor woman who would never know, until it was too late, that she had crossed a mean girl. But I said nothing. I simply made a mental note that this was a group of women I would try to avoid, and I would until that day when two of them were sitting across my desk.

The 'leader' had traded her white tennis dress for tight jeans held together by a perfect line of safety pins. The gap allowed a sliver of bright red underwear to peek out, accessorizing the look, I guess. The jeans were topped off by a pink silk blouse, four buttons undone, a black bra, no mystery. I admit I had never had anyone dress so Saturday night for a meeting in the mayor's office. What did her daughter think? Maybe nothing; was it just me? Her lieutenant was dressed in jeans and a blue tee shirt – so nondescript that I barely remember.

The three young girls had a prepared list of demands. I tried to buy time with the obligatory small talk; I was dying to know which girl went with which mom. They would not indulge me; okay, right to the problems at hand. "Do you even know what is happening in our country? You should be embarrassed that our city is such a mess!" Hmm, way to start a conversation that leads nowhere. The meeting was worse than a B movie. The girls were not interested in listening, discussing, or heaven forbid, learning. This was not about accomplishing anything, this was about showing me total disrespect and demanding their way by being belligerent. I started watching the clock, they had 30 minutes.

What were the two mothers doing during the girl's lecture? Mean girl was nodding along and taking every pause as her chance to jump in, adding fuel to the fire. Her lieutenant was looking down the entire time, too embarrassed or afraid to engage. Both mothers were enablers. I looked over at them several times. Something? Anything? Finally, when the lieutenant politely asked her daughter to try to be calm, her daughter snapped, "You aren't part of this." That was it for me; their time was up – 23 minutes. I remained gracious but incensed as I escorted them out. The teens showed up angry and left angry. Their dutiful mothers scurried out behind them.

The young women were comfortable talking down to me because they felt entitled. Sorry, your child is not entitled to be right. That behavior is taught by parents who are afraid of setting boundaries. It is your child who loses if you allow them to raise their voice until they get what they want. There is a reason we are called parents, not buddies. Those three girls could have learned a great deal if they had been willing to listen and ask questions rather than lecture. They would still have left angry, but none of us get our way all the time, usually because we do not have all the facts. When you prejudge, you will always find an adversary. You must master basic life skills like the art of conversation, debate, simple disagreement, and respecting other opinions. Parents are throwing their children to the wolves without these skills. Trust me, no one will ever love your child as much as you do. Do not teach them to be selfish, entitled, disrespectful, and mean.

Years earlier, I wondered why those three women were willing to take marching orders so dutifully. I had my answer. One woman was the perfect follower, she sought out a mean girl to give her directions, and now her daughter and her daughter's friends were treating her the same way. It made me feel blue; I love a good debate; it is food for the soul, but I am grateful my parents taught me respect. Granted, I learned a few lessons the hard way. Haven't we all? That is the job of parents. A poor woman named 'her' reminded me how dangerous it is to be a follower, to allow yourself to be used by a mean girl. Respect yourself; you deserve friends who will lift you up, show grace and understanding, and forgive you rather than pay you back.

Do not be a mother who would rather lose friends than face reality. Many years ago, I was involuntarily put in the middle of a parent child situation. I was a city councilwoman at the time, and it was not unusual to receive phone calls from residents wanting to pass on information anonymously – usually neighbor disputes. I received a phone call from a lady who confided that the teenage daughter of a woman I knew was sneaking out of the house in the middle of the night. The families lived on the same street, the anonymous caller had insomnia and noticed dim car lights creeping down her street at 2a.m. After a few nights, she decided to watch more closely, trying to figure out what was going on. The car would slow to a stop, and a girl would run across the street and meet the car. Regardless of what was going on, I thought that her mother would want to know. I called her; I assumed she would simply say thanks and hang up. I had no interest in asking any questions; this was just one parent watching out for another.

I certainly did not expect the reaction I got. The mother denied it could have happened and demanded to know who the 'snitch' was. She asserted that it was impossible. She demanded to know the color and type of car, where it stopped, and how the neighbor knew it was her daughter. I assured her that was all I had been told. Three days later, she called back even more upset. All she had done was stew over who the 'snitch' could be. Her daughter denied it, and mom believed her. I was so sorry I had 'done the right thing.' The car and the kid laid low for a few weeks; confident they had thrown everyone off the trail. The next time they met up, they got caught. The police were involved; the liaison was not harmless. That daughter knew her mother would always defend her, no matter what the situation. She watched her mother argue with friends, police, teachers, and neighbors. She watched her mother lose friends. If her mother did not value friendships, why should she? What kind of example had that mother mistakenly set for her daughter?

Chapter 12
Sticks and Stones

"You rarely see the struggles
in someone else's journey so
do not assume that their
path was easier than yours."

Ambitious, pushy, bossy, overbearing, intense, intimidating, and dare I say, bitchy. What successful woman has not been called one or more of these over the years? Or worse. I laugh when I recall a very naïve me, right out of college, starting out in the hospitality industry. I was cussed at, physically chased out of the kitchen during a busy dinner service, and had a chef throw a knife in my direction. Do not feel bad for me; I brought out the worst in many chefs, male and female. Professional women have been called everything, to our faces and behind our backs. Most are stereotypical, and all are demeaning. But if we get branded, whether we deserve it or not, our reputation resume can be damaged. Sexist? It can be, but too often it is other women elbowing us, labeling us, and creating obstacles to our success. Boys ignore us, girls score us; it is the playground mindset. Women can often be too emotional for their own good, and it costs us much of our power. Whether you are too intense or too tearful, you will be judged. An overload of any emotion in the workplace is a yellow flashing light – danger ahead – an excuse to be sidestepped, overlooked, and overjudged. No matter what results we achieve, we never get credit without some qualification about how challenging we can be.

As a woman with a strong personality and intense character, I get branded all the time, most often by other women. Our efforts to be overprepared, professional, and in control come across as intimidating. We spend years climbing the ladder, trying to figure out what men want without alienating women, only to end up in an unwinnable tug of war. Modeling yourself after the men in your workplace is the path many women take. The temptation is understandable because most of the success we see around us is achieved by men. It is not something we like to talk about, but we watch successful men, and try to mimic their style, their habits. Women are notorious for wanting to be included in the group, even if men are writing the rules. We are all familiar with the good ole boys club, but not the good ole girls club. Women have a harder time managing female relationships in the workplace than men. Even when you think you have a solid relationship with a female co-worker, you can be surprised.

A friend shared with me a recent story told to her by one of her female clients. The client was a successful corporate director who was part of a team of ten – two women and eight men. They had worked together for four years, and she considered them trusted colleagues. The client recently received a big promotion. Co-workers from throughout the company sent congratulations and best wishes. When she arrived at work the next day, her fellow team members cheered and clapped with balloons and a 'Nothing Bundt Cake.' Even the plates and napkins proclaimed congratulations! One director was noticeably missing – the only other woman on the team. The absent colleague wandered in a half hour late, looked at the party leftovers, and announced, "Oh, I'm sorry, I forgot." Yes, she had been on the group text the evening before to plan the festivities. She just could not help herself; she sent a message loud and clear: "Sorry, I forgot." The problem is that she sent the message to everyone on the team; she let envy get the better of her. I am guessing her male co-workers looked at her a bit differently moving forward.

The smallest amount of effort can mean the most. It is really about supporting each other in simple ways and being there when it matters. Never forget that women who have achieved big things have failed too. You rarely see the struggles in someone else's journey, so do not assume that their path was easier than yours. As you are climbing your ladder, watch, listen, and ask lots of questions. Copy the best and learn from the worst. Be open to sharing the lessons you have learned. Sometimes the opportunity to mentor pops up in unexpected places.

I had a 21-year-old meet with me about a possible summer internship in local government; actually her mother set the meeting up, which was my first red flag. The young woman was a rising college senior majoring in urban planning. Lovely young woman, a great student with an impressive resume. After the niceties, I asked about her future plans and what kind of experience she was hoping to gain from an internship. Pretty basic or so I thought. She replied, "The internship is a requirement for my major, but I need flexible hours because I have an online therapy group that meets every Tuesday and Friday morning, and I never miss. I don't understand how women can operate without therapy. Do you go to therapy?" I have never been asked that question, much less by someone who is asking me to help them find a job. If you need, want, or enjoy therapy, good for you, but it is not something you need to share in an interview. She changed the entire trajectory of our meeting. She was more passionate talking about the value of therapy than her future career plans. This was a mentoring moment. I was fairly certain that she would not have asked the same question if I was a man. I was right. I gave her some advice. I do not know if it resonated with her; maybe someday it will. Yes, I was honest and told her that it is important to know your audience. Yes, I asked her if she had considered changing her major.

Sometimes the best lessons come from the worst examples. I had a boss in my 20s whose only requirement was that I be on time every day. He stated, "It is not my job to cover for you or tell you what to do." He never asked me any questions because he did not need or want anything from me. I remember coming to work one day on time, and he was gone. We had a new manager who had much higher expectations, imagine that. It was a huge struggle for the entire staff because eight months of zero leadership hurt everyone's performance. We had languished without direction or goals. The old boss was in the perfect position to be a mentor; I was one of the 'up and coming' young managers, but he was not willing to make any effort to mentor me. With no one to push me, I learned to accept mediocrity because I was 23. And isn't that what 23-year-olds do? We must expect more from people for them to learn. We must be pushed to feel the pull. Those eight months may have been easy, but they hurt my career growth and taught me a valuable lesson: if no one is willing or able to challenge you, find friends and colleagues who will. If that does not work, do it yourself. Take responsibility for challenging yourself. Lesson learned. It took me months to recover and get back on track. Accepting mediocracy trains people to be ordinary.

Do not be afraid to shake up your normal. Every successful woman has experienced phases where she feels stuck. One of the ways I have shaken things up over the years is by challenging myself to stand in the back of the room. We work hard to get to the front of the room, so why would we choose to stand in the back of the room? Why? Because every organization looks much different to those whose view is from the back. They are the folks that are low on the totem pole, not part of the leadership team, or, in some organizations, not one of the cool kids. We work hard to get to the front, but once there, do not forget about what is going on behind you.

I gave a speech about leadership to a large business group. The room was full of successful business owners, operators, and city leaders. I started my speech front and center behind the big podium, and I proceeded to take the microphone and walk to the back of the packed banquet room. "Today, I am going to speak from the back of the room because I want everyone to look at their workplace, organization, philanthropy, or any group they lead from a completely different perspective. You walked into this luncheon today and took your seats with your comfortable connections. Three reserved tables are up front – in effect, the seats of honor and closest to the speaker. Now I am in the back of the room, where the folks who thought they could sneak out early or spend their time texting are seated. Well, not today, today we are going to shake up the status quo."

Always look for ways to shake up your normal. I was asked to be a model in a charity fashion show hosted by a local women's club. I desperately wanted to say no because the idea of walking a runway in front of 400 women was terrifying. The fashion show organizer asked for my contact information and said she would reach out to me to schedule the clothing fitting. Honestly, I hoped she would misplace my number. This was so far out of my comfort zone. I love the stage but prefer to be behind a podium (holding on). Practice what you preach. If someone gives you a chance to push yourself, take it.

After the event, the 'models' (regular ladies like me, all willing to step out of their comfort zone) posted fun pictures from the event; it was a day of camaraderie, meeting new friends, and reconnecting with old ones. One of the 'models,' a local business owner and member of the club, posted a message that really shows the value of reaching out of your comfort zone. After congratulating the club, she talked about the good work they do and the fun members have; then she added, "If you would like to come to our next monthly luncheon, message me. I would love for you to join me as my guest." Taking that extra step to reach out and offer a path to another woman who may be nervous about walking into a new group says as much about the club as the member who posted. We all know what those butterflies feel like, and they are never as bad when we have someone to join us when we walk in.

'Sticks and stones may break my bones, but names will never hurt me.' Well, I beg to differ. Words hurt, especially when they are meant to land a blow. I have spoken to many women who are so terrified by the mean girls that they suffer in silence or gradually stop showing up. Women hate confrontations, and if you push back against a mean girl, or worse, a mean girl clique, you will face backlash. I have spoken to women who were bullied in some of the 'feel-good' groups. The cruelty is painful; the attacks are meant to embarrass and humiliate – smart, attractive (on the outside) women ganging up on a woman who made the mistake of drawing their ire. If you choose to be a silent observer because you fear the mean girls, you are empowering them, and someday you may be the unfortunate target. It does not matter if you are shy or outspoken; they circle around and push you out. Run.

No, not every group is a perfect fit for everyone, but targeting members is a deal-breaker. Put yourself in places that give you opportunities to meet women who share your values; it may lead to a cup of coffee, lunch, a new acquaintance, or even friendship. I was the guest speaker at a self-described mom group several years ago. The meeting started with the club president reminding all the members, "You are welcome here in your pajamas, with baby throw up on your shoulder or cracker crumbs in your hair." I loved that; they were just glad you made it, no judgment. Your time is a gift, so never discount the value that you bring to every group you join.

When I served as mayor, I became painfully aware of the amount of time I was volunteering. I mentally sorted through the job responsibilities versus the nice-to-do things. Balancing a business, family, and the non-paying mayor position forced me to prioritize; something had to give, so I decided to give where I got back. You get to be selfish, to give to the things, and people, that fill your soul. It is much like being in business and deciding where to best spend the little extra time you have outside of the office. Yes, philanthropy is important, but I am the first to admit that sometimes I would rather donate rather than volunteer to work an event. When I was younger, I could not afford to write checks and was happy to donate my time instead. Your time and treasure have tremendous value; be sure you know that and only give what you are comfortable giving.

Above all else, before you give, make sure you know what defines a good match for you. Is your goal personal or professional? Most professional women join groups to network, build connections, gain knowledge, and develop future clients. It is rewarding to bond over shared interests and hobbies. Where you donate your time and treasure and the causes you are passionate about make you bigger than being the local insurance agent, realtor, banker, or carpet cleaning company. You are selling yourself, and that means you have to relate beyond your position, your company, and the service you provide. Volunteering together and bonding through shared causes builds much deeper connections.

Maybe because I am older and wiser, I appreciate easy friendships and gravitate toward relaxed organizations. I know my worth, and I am way past the stage of life where I have any interest in pretending things are not what they are. I want to be around honest women, perfect in their imperfection, because being fake never gets anyone anything they really want. The years have taught me some tried-and-true tips that will help you maximize the time you give when you have no time.

1. Walk into every room looking for someone to whom you can say something positive.

   It puts a smile on your face and gives you a shot of energy. Knowing that the next thing out of your mouth will be positive takes your mind off the butterflies we all get. It is a great icebreaker when you do not know many people at an event. Do not feel pressured to make small talk; sometimes a nice comment does not spark much more than a smile or nod.

2. Never miss an opportunity to make an introduction.

   Welcome others into your conversation by being aware when someone seems to be standing close, waiting to speak to you. Take a step back and turn your shoulder slightly toward them, opening the door, to welcome them into the conversation. The folks you are speaking to will notice your movement, so follow it up quickly with an introduction. I try to steer clear of serious conversations at events, so this will also help you from getting cornered. The introduction will be appreciated, and often a new group dynamic forms. This allows you to excuse yourself to keep working the room. Do not worry if you are terrible with names. When you welcome a new person into the conversation pause and ask if they know everyone. Nine times out of ten they will extend their hand, and offer their name, and so will everyone else.

3. Do not underestimate the power of a compliment.

Planned compliments do not have to be fake. Social media is a great source to stay up-to-date on what the people you will be seeing are up to. Whether it is a recent trip, promotion, anniversary, or a new grandchild, there is always a way to connect in a meaningful way. I keep a little Rolodex in my head.

4. Do what you must do in 20 minutes.

This is my favorite tip. We cannot do it all, but what do we do when we must make an appearance? You get in and out in 20 minutes, period. First, find the organizer and beeline it to them. They need to know that you were there, or you wasted your effort. Circle the room. Make a complete loop and keep your eyes and feet moving. Touch base with as many people as you can; keep yourself limited to a wave, a nod with a smile, or a quick hello, nice to see you, as you shake hands and keep moving. If anyone tries to corner you, hand them your card and ask them to give you a call. Once I have looped the entire room, I head in the direction of the exit, but take a different route through the room. This helps you see different people than on your first run through. There are key people at any event, and you will want to be sure to make eye contact with them if you cannot get close enough to shake hands. You cannot be at every event from start to finish; it is up to you to prioritize who gets your time. I have attended luncheons and only stayed for the pre-lunch networking, and I have gone to dinners and only stayed for the cocktail hour. You do what you have to do.

Busy women are constantly faced with choices. We choose friends, professions, hobbies, what we value, where we spend our time, and with whom. It is not always easy to find the place where we belong, but there is tremendous value in the journey. Accept who you are but strive to be the best version of yourself. Surround yourself with women who appreciate you as much as you appreciate them. Do you have time for anything less? I feel fortunate to have had loyal women in my life who have stuck with me. Becoming a public official while still running a business took so much of my time and energy. What was left had to go to my family. There were days that I did not have anything left for anyone else. I have talked to women who are in positions of tremendous responsibility, and they say the same thing; friendships suffer first. But what surprised and disappointed them the most were the girlfriends who drifted away when they started to achieve big things.

True friends support each other whether it is high tide or low tide. The key is to stay connected. Find small but thoughtful ways to show that you value their friendship. Pinterest is a great resource. I bought some hand designed notecards from a local artist in my town, and once or twice a year I will drop a quick note just to say hi! The friends who matter will wait for you, but never take them for granted.

Living in Texas, we rarely get 'pretty' snow and never at Christmastime. In 2012, we woke up Christmas morning to a snow globe world; the wonderland did not last long. It never does in Texas. A few weeks later a card came in the mail with a picture of our house covered in white. Inside was a note from a dear friend. She and her husband drove around early Christmas morning, taking pictures of their friends' homes, all decorated in snowy white draping with not a footprint in sight. I cherish the thoughtfulness. Another friend is an avid gardener, her daffodils and irises are magnificent every April when they bloom. I came home from work one day to find a small paper bag on my front porch. When she divided her bulbs, she made gift bags filled with bulbs for her friends, a simple note on the bag, 'thinking of you!' Now I look forward to my own gorgeous yellow daffodils and deep purple irises blossoming every spring. I smile and think of her. Both women are still my dear friends. It is the little things that keep the connections strong. Learn from the kindness others show you.

Chapter 13

Find Your Dinner Group

"Mean girls will never be part
of a group that stays together;
they need constant change,
new targets."

Y ou cannot have a genuine connection, much less a true friendship, without trust. Anyone who has ever sat around a table
with friends, acquaintances, colleagues, or strangers knows how
different you feel when there is established trust and when there is
not. Everyone needs a dinner group. Call it what you want; come

together for whatever reason, but everyone needs to gather around a table with people they deeply trust and care for. Like an old family recipe, honesty, laughter, empathy, and loyalty are stirred together and baked with heart. If you follow the recipe without skipping a step, you will create something incredible – a feast for your soul. The time you spend around the table fills you up; friends giving their best and receiving the best in return. We all need friendships worth celebrating, brought together for dozens of different reasons. It is about investing in people with the goal of deepening connections, building trust, and forming lifelong relationships. Be intentional and find your dinner group.

Making friends takes effort and requires an investment in your social wellbeing. Choosing correctly can only be learned by trial and error. Be true to yourself first; followers tend to attract women who dominate them, so do not be a follower. Never assume everyone else already has their own friend group; they do not. Too many women are lonely because they assume other women are only looking for the funniest, smartest, cutest, and most clever women with whom to be friends. We are all looking, hoping, and feeling a bit insecure about the whole process. You have to ask for friendship so seek out what interests you and find places where you enjoy spending your time. Join an organization, a sport, an association, or a club. If you love reading, get involved in your local library; join the board. If you have a green thumb, join your local garden club. Give it your best effort; offer your time, volunteer, host, and get engaged. Commit.

Familiarity is a magnet for friendship. You will naturally meet potential friends by spending time with like-minded women. Offer a compliment or comment on a great event. A positive comment tells people you want to connect. Do not be afraid to invite another woman or group of women you want to get to know for a cup of coffee. For younger moms, host a playdate. If you love needlework, put together a stitching group. If you like to walk, put an invite on social media for interested women to meet up. Groups become your community. You do not have to host at your home, meet at local restaurants, parks, a recreation center or a favorite coffee shop. Do not let location hold you back. Consistent group gatherings sow the seeds of friendship. Yes, it is awkward, but you have to ask for friendship. Get out of your comfort zone, and you will move away from unhealthy friendships and find women who make you feel valued. Believe me, mean girls are not willing to put in the work; they only have time to invest in themselves.

We have been taught since we were little girls that we should have a lot of friends. Certainly, the popular girls do, don't they? We have the habit of using the word friend flippantly. The word slides easily off the tongue, often with bare shelves to back it up. It is hard to categorize every relationship, and easier to casually roll them all together. Friend is a happy word that presumes there is a meaningful relationship, even when there is not. As we grow up, we realize it is not about a number; it is about quality. I have never lost a trusted friend, but I have been fooled into thinking a woman was a friend when she was not – my error. I refer to it as investing in the long term with a person who only invests in the short term. A bad investment is a bad investment; we have all made those blunders.

1. Friendship is earned; it is an investment of your time and heart.

2. Do not be afraid to ask for friendship.

3. Do not wait to be invited, be an inviter.

4. Show appreciation, write thank you notes, remember important occasions.

5. Find communities of shared interests and be consistent in participating.

Everyone in my dinner group is devoted to the group and the meaning it carries for each of us. We all look forward to being together around the table, laughing, sharing, listening, planning, and laughing some more. It takes effort in our busy lives to prioritize our time together. But when we pull our chairs up to the table, we are reminded how treasured our time together is and how hard you must work to prioritize the friendships that are most important to you. We have invested in each other. We share a history, memories, good times, and bad. Time is a rare commodity; spend it wisely. It is why humans cherish genuine friendship and are wounded by false friendship. Genuine friendship thrives due to the uniqueness we each bring to every endeavor. Many women think the easiest way forward is to give away some of their uniqueness. Do not make that mistake. You owe yourself friendships based on reality, not fantasy. Surround yourself with friends and colleagues who are happy for your successes and supportive of you when you have failures. Never give your power away or sell yourself short just to earn a friend; it will not last, and it will hurt when it ends. Mean girls will never be part of a group that stays together long-term; they need constant change and new targets.

Friendships with men and women alike are essential, but women must be the biggest cheerleaders for other women. We must encourage other women by recognizing their achievements. Be there with a compliment, not judgment. Mentoring other women is so important to the future successes for which we all strive. It is still a battle for us to get to the top, but when we do, we must reach down to pull other women up with us. Unfortunately, once we fight our way to the top, we often hunker down, protecting our turf.

During my 14 years in corporate America, 25 years owning a business, and 14 years serving in elected office, I have been very fortunate to have met dozens of smart, confident, and successful women. They are women I admire and aspire to be more like. Years ago, one of the women I have always looked up to unexpectedly left a successful corporate career in which she had invested almost two decades. I first noticed her career change on social media. I had not recalled her being a frequent poster, but suddenly she seemed to be everywhere, doing everything in her industry – attending conferences, luncheons, and retreats. There was no other word for it: she was radiating joy; her outfits were brighter, her smile wider, she was happy, and it was infectious. I was excited when we ran into each other at a women's leadership event. We hugged and quickly got caught up – kids, husbands, dogs. She invited me over to her table to meet her coworkers, who exuded positivity. I felt welcomed. She had found the place where she fit.

A few weeks later, I reached out and invited her to grab a cup of coffee. Before I took the first sip of my lavender latte, I blurted out, "What happened? You had it all?" Looking back, I could have been a bit more skilled, but I was gobsmacked. How did she get from there to here? A touch of melancholy moved over her face. A woman had been promoted to head her division; it was a very prestigious job. While the 'mostly male' corporation was patting itself on the back, first woman this, first woman that, the other females in the organization knew that this was a woman who pulled the ladder up.

She was known as 'one of the guys' because she worked so well with the male executives but had a track record of being reluctant to put women in key positions on her team. My friend realized it was time to pivot; she knew her value and saw the reality of how this new boss would affect her future. She was not alone; over time, the women who could left too.

For years now, my friend has been a top executive who never pulls the ladder up. She is a connector, a supporter of women, and one of my most valued mentors. Reflecting on her career change and subsequent success reminds me how important it is to always face forward. Never stop asking yourself, What next? Women executives at every level need to be mentors – women who support other women and are willing to work toward shared goals. Mean girls are only motivated by their own goals; once you help them achieve those goals, they will pull the ladder up. If you find yourself working for a mean girl, be ready to pivot.

Many female professionals fall victim to the good ole boys club. There is too much pressure on women to be like men because women have watched for years as the road to success is jammed with men. Many women think that is the easiest way forward, so they give away some of their uniqueness and make the significant mistake of trying to be like men in their professional lives. Challenge yourself to be a woman who actively looks for an opportunity to compliment another woman. Be a team-builder, not a one-woman show. Reach out to women in different industries, women who can teach you; be a mentor, and find a mentor. Always use your own voice and stand behind your words. Whether you are speaking, writing a letter or email, having a casual conversation, or posting on social media, be thoughtful and classy. Do not give your power away by confusing how you feel with what you want to achieve.

You can learn the biggest lessons in the simplest places. I am a fantastic gift wrapper. My packages have the most beautiful corners because of the woman who ran the gift wrap department at Bowman's Department Store in Camp Hill, Pennsylvania. I was home for Christmas break during my freshman year in college. I worked the candy counter at Bowman's during high school, but the gift-wrapping department was slammed, and I was the 'kid' and low man on the totem pole, so I was reassigned. The department looked like a tornado had hit. There were piles of bags and boxes as far as the eye could see, not to mention a line of customers tensely waiting for their free Christmas wrapping. Where to begin? Like many kids, I helped my mom wrap presents for relatives every Christmas, so I jumped right in. The head of gift-wrapping was clearly not excited about getting stuck with some kid. To her credit, she never left my side, kindly guiding me and repeating the same instructions a dozen times, praying I would catch on. That first weekend, she wrapped right next to me, checking my work. She trained me not to rush or take shortcuts. I was given the gift of time and attention. Have pride in a job well done, no matter how small, and be willing to teach others with the same patience and pride. I feel that pride every time I wrap a gift, and my packages reflect it.

1. Absorb every teachable moment.

2. Have pride in a job well done.

3. Pay attention to the small things; you could learn something big.

4. If help is offered, take it.

5. Never cut corners, it will show.

Like a perfectly wrapped present, friendship is a gift that deserves your best effort. It takes being intentional, which requires discipline. First, be clear on what your most important priorities are. Second, be honest with yourself. Who is getting most of your energy, and does that list align with your top priorities? Women are not always good at saying no. Instead, we overextend, overdo, and exhaust ourselves by doing too much but never enough. Take the rose-colored glasses off; it may hurt when you see the imbalance in some of your relationships, but it is better to know. Your best energy should go to those who treat you the same in return. I do not regret the mean friends, the dreadful bosses, or the personal missteps. All the women I invited to lunch—the ladies I admire most—said the same thing. They are tough and self-aware. Women who stand behind every decision they make, good or bad. They own their stuff, and their confidence is infectious.

6. Not everyone is going to like you.

7. Not everyone is going to invite you.

8. Do not purposely leave people out.

9. The people that give their best should get your best.

10. Friendship requires your best, so be intentional.

Women prefer the comfort of a reliable female friend group; it is safe and predictable. It takes me back to my days in high school. We love our cliques, popular or not. We must challenge ourselves to walk into new spaces. A fulfilled life needs constant learning, fresh ideas, and unique experiences, even from those who see things differently than we do. It is vital to learn from other women. You do not have to become fast friends, but we miss out on so many opportunities to thrive because we are not willing to connect with women outside of our cliques. No woman should miss out on the wisdom other women can share. We can all benefit from understanding another woman's journey. I have a dear friend who always says, "My friend card is full; I have all the real friends I need." Gosh, I finally feel like I am at the age where I can say I am sick of fake friends who do nothing but take up space. The worst are the women who smile to our faces when we know what they say behind our backs. Women who intentionally and consciously treat you badly but believe that a fake grin and a "So glad to see you, how are things going?" would mislead you. I actually watched one of these women corner my husband at an event with her insincere interest. Seriously? Sorry, I no longer feel any obligation to pretend. If you choose to hang around people who totally disrespect me, you do not get to play act with me. If I am not good enough for you to defend when you are with your mean friends, then why do you want to be sweet when they are not around? If you are a woman who thinks it is easier to play along, consider the time you are wasting that could be spent with real friends.

11. Judge people by how they treat others, including you, when you are not around.

12. Stay clear of the drama.

13. Being fake speaks volumes about your character.

14. If you are not strong enough to defend a friend, you do not deserve that friend.

15. If you choose being a follower over being decent, you will never find happiness.

Women are naturally gifted at making connections and solving problems. In public service, philanthropy, and business, we bring empathy and a way of communicating that is authentic and full of purpose. What holds us back is ourselves – fear, lack of confidence, a desire not to be judged, never throwing caution to the wind. When women come together with a shared purpose, they can do incredible things. Fourteen years ago, I was invited to lunch with five women who were determined to make meaningful change in our community. Our goal was in part to combat an 'exclusive' (their word, not mine) fraternity-style organization in our community where, at the time, a small group of moms selected and rejected high school mothers and sons with zero (or secret) rhyme or reason. The moms who invited me to lunch believed high school was no place for this kind of selection process, and rather than complain, they rolled up their sleeves. Eight mothers and our eight high school sons established 'Scholars and Athletes Serving Others'. S.A.S.O. is an inclusive service organization that has gone on to welcome thousands of mothers and their high school sons. The organization also embraced the need for a mother-daughter division, and both have thrived and continue to grow.

What are we teaching our young sons and daughters when we, as mothers, decide to pick and choose who is in and who is out? The four years my son and I spent doing community service together are some of my best memories of his high school days. The organization is mighty and continues to make an enormous impact on the lives of those in need and the dozens of local charities they have offered their services to. Thousands of young men and women have volunteered tens of thousands of hours side by side with their mothers, making new friends and putting others first. What an amazing gift:

learning by doing. Our goal as mothers should be to raise our sons and daughters to be decent human beings who value giving back. I cannot imagine my community without those women gathered around a table, determined to create a service organization where every high school child who wanted to join would be welcome. For four years, through our sons' freshman, sophomore, junior, and senior years, we worked side by side to make meaningful change. Eight families saw something wrong and decided to make it right. I am so proud to have those women in my life.

It is 2 p.m., and I am sitting in Harvest Hall overlooking the trains as they pull in and out of the Main Street Station. It is a busy day, and the trains provide an ever-changing backdrop. I love this spot. This is where I began to write, and this is where I will write my last chapter. I order a large lavender latte at The Main Line Coffee Bar. When the young woman hands it to me, I smile and thank her for the perfect foamy heart on top, a good sign. I wander over to my favorite spot, excited that the best table overlooking the train station is free – another good sign. My mind begins to wander. It has been doing that more and more because I know I am close to the end of writing this book. Part of me cannot wait to finish, but part of me dreads it being over. Finishing a book is like saying goodbye to a dear friend. For six months, we have been inseparable. Together, we have struggled and rejoiced. Oh, the joy of finding the perfect phrase! My mind drifts back to where I started: women must do better. We owe it to our daughters and our sons. We must take better care of ourselves and our friendships. We must be mentors, trusted colleagues, and caring friends. Surround yourself with friends that lift you up – people who care about you as much as you care about them. After I mentally type THE END, I click on my calendar app, anticipating all the free time I have to look forward to. I see a little dot on next Friday, dinner group at 7:30 p.m. I cannot think of a better way to celebrate.